Dr. Maroof Maqbool

Educational Developments in South Kashmir Since Indian Independence

Anchor Academic
Publishing

Maqbool, Maroof: Educational Developments in South Kashmir Since Indian Independence, Hamburg, Anchor Academic Publishing 2016

Buch-ISBN: 978-3-96067-095-7
PDF-eBook-ISBN: 978-3-96067-595-2
Druck/Herstellung: Anchor Academic Publishing, Hamburg, 2016

Bibliografische Information der Deutschen Nationalbibliothek:
Die Deutsche Nationalbibliothek verzeichnet diese Publikation in der Deutschen Nationalbibliografie; detaillierte bibliografische Daten sind im Internet über http://dnb.d-nb.de abrufbar.

Bibliographical Information of the German National Library:
The German National Library lists this publication in the German National Bibliography. Detailed bibliographic data can be found at: http://dnb.d-nb.de

© Anchor Academic Publishing, Imprint der Diplomica Verlag GmbH
Hermannstal 119k, 22119 Hamburg
http://www.diplomica-verlag.de, Hamburg 2016
Printed in Germany

CONTENTS

INTRODUCTION

Introduction

By education we mean the natural, harmonious and progressive development of man`s innate powers by drawing out the best in his body, mind and spirit so as to produce an individual who is culturally refined, emotionally stable, ethically sound, mentally alert, morally upright, physically strong, socially efficient, spiritually enlightened, vocationally self-sufficient and internationally liberal. This should be the end product of education. Any programme of education which puts exclusive emphasis on one of these aspects of the human personality will be considered as lop-sided and narrow. Broadly speaking, this functional and operational definition and meaning should guide us in planning and implementing our educational programmes. The process of education begins immediately after the child is born. His mother teaches him how to breast feed. By using trial and error technique, the child comes to learn how to suck milk from the breast of the mother. As a child`s exposure expands, the number of his formal and informal teachers also increases. This process continues till his/her last breath in some way or the other. Thus, whole life of man is centred on his/her wisdom or intelligence making him superior to all other living being in the process.

Education has a fundamental role to play in personal and social development and is an indispensable asset to confront the many challenges that the future holds in store for mankind. Education attempts to attain the ideals of peace, freedom and social justice. It is one of the principal means to foster a deeper and more harmonious form of human development and thereby to reduce poverty, exclusion, ignorance, oppression and war.

The basic aim of education is to develop the potential of an individual in the best possible way. Education is also regarded as a conscious effort and process that brings about desired changes in the human beings. Education not only refers to the acquisition of 3R's namely reading, writing and arithmetic but when perceived in a broader sense, education refers to the multidimensional development of an individual. The role of education in facilitating social and economic progress is well recognised. It opens up opportunities leading to both individual and group entitlements. Education in its broadest sense of development of youth is the most crucial input for empowering people with skills and knowledge and giving them access to productive employment in future.

Education is the most powerful means of social, political and economic change. It works like an instrument in bringing desirable changes for overall development of the nation. In a democratic country like India with vast cultural, social, religious and linguistic diversities, providing equal educational opportunities is a real big task. In the present globalization the world is shrunk to a global village and every society is the member of the village. So every member has to keep pace with the educational developments in this village. In the absence of it the societies will lag behind in the process of development.

Education can be achieved through informal, non-informal and formal ways. The informal education is achieved from nature without any conscious efforts and is a lifelong process. Non-formal education is not acquired through formal institutions but through some media like radio, television, internet, computers, audio-video cassettes and printed media etc. The formal education is imparted through conscious, deliberate process in order to achieve predetermined set of educational objectives. This process takes place in the formal institutions like schools and colleges and an attempt is made to develop the cognitive and affective domains as well as some psychomotor skills. For formal education, school plays a very important role in developing and shaping the individuals. It is now generally felt that school education should aim all round development of the child's personality by rebuilding the four pillars of learning i.e. learning to know, learning to do, learning to live together and learning to be.

Education in India is provided by the public sector as well as the private sector, with control and funding coming from three levels: central, state, and local. Takshasila was the earliest recorded centre of higher learning in India from at least 5th century B.C and it is debatable whether it could be regarded a university or not. The Nalanda University was the oldest university system of education in the world in the modern sense of university. Western education became ingrained into Indian society with the establishment of the British Raj.

Education in India falls under the control of both the union government and the state governments, with some responsibilities lying with the union and the states having autonomy for others. The various articles of the Indian constitution provide for education as a fundamental right. Most of the universities in India are controlled by the union or the state governments.

India has made progress in terms of increasing the primary education attendance rate and expanding literacy to approximately three quarters of the population in the 7-10 age groups, by 2011. India's improved education system is often cited as one of the main contributors to the economic rise of India. Much of the progress, especially in higher education and scientific research, has been credited to various public institutions. At primary, upper primary, high school and higher level technical schools, India has a combination of public and private school system. About 60% of the students go to public schools and 40% to private; the private education market in India is generating revenue of US$ 450 million as per the data of the year 2008. As per the Annual Status of Education Report (ASER) 2012, 96.5% of all rural children between the ages of 6-14 were enrolled in schools. This is the fourth annual survey to report enrolment above 96%. Another report from 2013 stated that there were 229 million students enrolled in different accredited urban and rural schools of India, from class I to XII, representing an increase of 2.3 million students over 2002 total enrolment, and a 19% increase in girl's enrolment. While quantitatively India is moving closer to universal education, the quality of its education has been questioned particularly in its government run school system. One of the reasons for the poor quality includes absence of around 25% of the teachers every day. States of India have introduced tests and education assessment system to identify and improve such schools.

Overview

India's education system is divided into different levels such as pre-primary level, primary level, elementary education, secondary education, undergraduate level and postgraduate level. The National Council of Educational Research and Training (NCERT) and The Central Board of Secondary Education (CBSE) are the two important apex bodies responsible for curriculum related matters of school education in India. The NCERT provides support and technical assistance to a number of schools in India and oversees many aspects of enforcement of educational policies.

In addition, NUEPA (National University of Educational Planning and Administration) and NCTE (National Council for Teacher Education) are responsible for the management of the education system and teacher accreditation.

Historical background of education in the state of Jammu and Kashmir

Jammu and Kashmir State as a single political entity was founded by Maharaja Gulab Singh under the Treaty of Amritsar signed by him with the British Government in March 1846, with slight modifications thereafter agreed to by both. Before that all the four regions of the state, viz, Jammu, Kashmir, Ladakh and Gilgit had passed through centuries of vicissitudes mapping their individual historical courses and different parts and principalities had third distinct socio-political character. So, it was the state of education in these areas. In a discussion of the history of educational issues and problems of J&K state, it would therefore be reasonable to start from the year 1846. Even a brief description of the educational development in the state prior to this year would involve tracing the history of many an independent and fast changing kingdoms, which is outside the scope of this work. There is no doubt that the Kashmir has been the seat of learning since ancient times. The learned people of Kashmir have proved the credentials of their learning within and outside the country. Kalhana, in his Rajtarangni, which is the first ever written history, states about the significance that the people of Kashmir attached to learning. Sanskrit learning centers (universities) such as Vijeshwara and Sharda were famous for centuries. To achieve the knowledge in Sanskrit literature, story writing, politics, mathematics, poetry, drama, astrology and medicine people from the sub-continent thronged these learning centers. Kashmir was centres of Buddhism during Kanishka's rule and had the privilege of conducting fourth Buddhist council in the first century. During Muslim rule *Makatabs*, *Madarasas* and *Patshalas* were founded, where both Sanskrit and Persian were taught. During Zain-ul-Abideen's (popularly known as Budshah) rule a university was-founded at Srinagar. This was followed by a lull in the educational developments till Akbar conquered

Kashmir and the system geared up. After 1752, under Afghan rule the system showed signs of decline for seventy years. This was followed by further decline under the Sikh rule of Maharaja Ranjit Singh.

Thus, under the tyrant rulers of Kashmir, once an abode of learning was showing a declining trend in the educational field till the state of Jammu and Kashmir came into existence in1846. With Maharaja Gulab Singh as a ruler of Jammu and Kashmir the educational system started its revival with particular stress on art and literature. Maharaja Ranbir Singh, pious son of Maharaja Gulab Singh, being a lover of learning and art, paid special attention towards Sanskrit literature. He started first printing press-the *Vidya Vilas* Press, in the state for printing of books. He got many books translated into various languages through translation bureau founded by him. However, the education was still provided through the Makatabs and Patshalas. It was only due to the efforts of Christian Missionaries that the modern schooling started in the state. Thus the efforts made by the missionaries in establishing modern education system compelled the Maharaja of the state to open the schools on modern lines. Numbers of missionary private schools are still running in the state outclassing other private and government schools in the education standards. Last Dogra ruler of Kashmir Maharaja Hari Singh took personal interest in the expansion of education in the state. In 1938, education committee under the chairmanship of Mr. K. G. Saiyidan recommended the introduction of the basic education or Wardha Scheme. Mr. Saiyidan was appointed Director of Education and directed to implement these recommendations. After independence numbers of education committees were formed to make the recommendations for re-organising and modernizing the educational system. The recommendations made from time to time were accepted by the government and implemented, resulting in the improvement of education in the state. Still, the government system was the major partner in educating the masses so the numbers of the private schools were less. But for last three decades the number of private schools has grown up to a considerable number of baffling imagination. With the political turmoil in late eighties the entire government system got disturbed with the education system being the worse hit. This disturbed government education system resulted in the mushroom growth of private primary schools in every nook and corner of the states besides already existing government system. This resulted in the decline of roll in the government schools to such an extent that dozens of government schools were closed due to lack of clientele. The opening of primary schools in the private sector is continuing at an alarming rate without any check.

With the partition of the country in 1947, the state leaders realized the significance of education and its importance for democracy. As such, it was imperative to begin with the process of development of education and formulating an education system suitable for the needs of society. At the time of independence, there were very few educational institutions in the state which were largely concentrated in the major towns. The state of affairs, as far as literacy is concerned, was such that the literacy rate of the state was very low at that time. This low level of literacy forced the state government to take serious note about the existing state of affairs and promote education in the state.

In 1947-1948 Sheikh Mohammad Abdullah of the Jammu and Kashmir National Conference was asked to form interim government in the state. Soon after taking over as first Prime Minister of the state, Sheikh Mohammad Abdullah retained the portfolio of Ministry of Education under his control. The taking over of education portfolio personally, by the Prime Minister was a recognition of the importance attached to education in the state. Sheikh Mohammad Abdullah started bringing reforms and revolutions in the 'old fashioned' system of education. Along with bringing the education system under its purview, however, the state found itself responsible for the education of its subjects; most of these were Muslims. Impetus was given to raise the general level of literacy as well as to provide adequate opportunities for primary, higher and technical education. In the opinion of Sheikh Mohammad Abdullah education for everyone was the basic need of the people if they were to emerge into enlightenment. Thus, efforts were made to bring a cardinal change in the old fashioned educational system and work on this was taken up with great enthusiasm. This resulted in the gradual expansion of institutions at all levels and their number started increasing but these efforts could not match up with the requirements.

On 17th November, 1956, the constitution of the state was adopted and enacted. Part IV Directive Principles of State Policy, clauses 20 to 23 contain following provisions pertaining to education:

Clause 20: Rights of free and compulsory education in certain cases.

The state shall endeavour:

a) To secure to every permanent resident the right to free education up to the university standard;

b) To provide, within a period of ten years from the commencement of this constitution, compulsory education for all children until they complete age of fourteen years; and

c) To ensure to all workers and employees adequate facilities for adult education and part-time technical, professional and vocational courses.

Clauses 21: Right of children:

The state shall strive to secure to all children and youth equal opportunities in education and employment.

Clause 22: Right of women:

The state shall endeavour to secure to all women;

The right to full equality in all social, educational, political and legal matters;

Clause 23: Protection of educational material and cultural interests of socially and economically backward sections.

Education system in Jammu and Kashmir

The political situation in Jammu and Kashmir is not very conducive to development of education or any other form of industry besides tourism. But nevertheless, the central and the state government authorities have tried their best to promote academics here. Free education is provided to students who come from poor families and cannot pay the fee for even primary education. The education system in Jammu and Kashmir is divided into the respective tiers namely primary, secondary and higher education besides the professional and technical education.

Need and importance of the study

Studies related with assessment and analysis of development of educational levels is very important from the socio-economic point of view. Such studies give us deeper insight of the actual and practical situation of the area of interest and become a base for future development in the system. Moreover, since rural areas are lagging behind in high educational level, such studies are much appreciated. Again the importance of such studies can be highlighted, as education is one of the measuring parameter of human development index. The investigator while scanning the literature found that no study have been conducted on the topic in Kashmir. The investigator found that the entire field is unexplored and after making in-depth study of different surveys, journals and other research inputs, it was found that no systematic study has been conducted which could objectively study the education and educational institutions in South Kashmir. The present investigation is an attempt to assess the education system and educational institutions which were prevalent in South Kashmir since 1948. The study shall be very useful for the planners and policy makers to frame educational polices for the people of Kashmir in general and South Kashmir in particular.

Rationale of the study

Education is a civilizational tool which discriminate human being from other animals. Right from the dawn of civilization, the man erected institutions to regulate their lives with peace, security and highest fulfilment of their potential and happiness. Educational institutions are the most potent one to achieve this goal.

The valley of Kashmir is located strategically in geographical terms. It abounds with beautiful natural endowments. The peculiar character of the state in terms of special status in the constitutional provision of India has given it more autonomy than other states. The people of Kashmir are very hard working and especially the population of South Kashmir is mostly engaged in horticulture and farming. It's beautiful natural resources and scenic beauty has been a greatest attraction for tourists from all over the World. The exposure of people of Kashmir with the outside World created a demand for establishing better institutions and especially educational institution at par with other states. The impact of globalization and liberalization has also influencing every aspect of life throughout the World. The valley of Kashmir cannot remain untouched with all these changes taking place all-round.

To deal with fast socio-economic changes, the educational institutions will have to develop and innovate itself to compete and cope up with the change. This scenario of change in society and the greater demand for competent, trained and qualified man power to manage the economic development driven by modern and sophisticated technology inspired the research to study this issue. The selection of the study area was based on the occupational nature of the people in this area which is characterised by agriculture and farming as the main source of income. The researcher tried to examine the chronological growth and development of educational institutions, the qualitative change in educational system and its impact on the people in terms of education at every level, health and employment in general terms.

This study was provided an overview of the development of educational institutions after independence under various regimes. It was also try to find out the grey areas in the system. This study will be of great help to planners and policy makers to understand this issue in proper perspective and motivate other researchers to carry this study forward.

Objectives of the study

The following objectives were formulated for the present study:

1. To study the various private and public institutions engaged in disseminating knowledge.
2. To study the changing policies of the state and various private institutions of education.
3. To study the causes behind the growth of private institutions.
4. To study the commonality and difference in the syllabus prescribed by the public and private institutions.
5. To study the sex-wise and rural-urban literacy growth.
6. To study the impact of education on the different structures of the society.

CHAPTER – II
REVIEW OF THE RELATED LITERATURE

Review of the Related Literature

The review of related literature gives the researcher an understanding of the research methodology which refers to the way of the study to be conducted. It helps the researcher to know about the tools and instruments which prove to be useful and promising in the previous studies. The advantage of the related literature is also to provide insight into statistical methods through which validity of results is to be established. By reviewing the related literature the researcher can avoid unfruitful and ineffective problem areas. He can select those areas in which positive findings are very likely to result and his/her endeavours would be likely to add to the knowledge in a meaningful way. The review of related literature enables the researcher to define the limits of her/his field. It helps the researcher to delimit and define her/his problem.

The knowledge of related literature brings the researcher up-to-date on the work which others have done and thus to state the objectives clearly and concisely. Through the review of related literature, the researcher can avoid unintentional duplication of well-established findings. It is no use to replicate a study when the stability and validity of its results have been clearly established. The final and important specific reason for reviewing the related literature is to know about the recommendations of the previous researchers for further research which they have listed in the studies. Helping in evaluating ones research efforts by providing a comparison, increasing ones confidence in choice of selected topic by viewing interest of others.

The accumulated research in all the disciplines for the last two decades has been accomplished a host of sub-areas with the result that the present day researchers seems to be altogether different from the studies, which were conducted in the past. Therefore, review of the previous literature for the development of objectively based hypotheses and enunciation of the new research design has become essential. The review of the educational literature gives educator an excellent overview of the work that has been done in the fields and helps him in keeping up with recent development. Review of the related literature also allows the researcher to acquaint himself with current knowledge in the field or area in which he is going to conduct his research. For a worthwhile research, the researcher needs to acquire up-to-date information relating to the problem, which is done through the review of the related literature. The survey of the related literature enables the investigator to locate the gaps and find the trends in the research tools employed by the other investigators helps the future investigators to state the problem; to weigh its significance, to work out data gathering devices suggest research design, to identify sources of data, to make effective statistical analysis, to arrive at potent conclusions and avoid duplication.

Knowledge of related literature enables the investigator to define the frontier of his field. It gives the researcher an understanding of the research methodology which refers to the way the study is to be conducted. It helps the researcher to know the tools and instruments which proved to be useful and promising in the previous studies. Therefore, the survey of such studies to a greater extent forewarns the prospective researcher about the most avowed research problem. It helps the researcher to delimit and define his problem and brings the researcher up-to-date on the work which others have done and thus to state the objectives clearly and concisely. By reviewing the related literature the researcher can avoid unfruitful useless problem areas. He can select those areas in which positive findings are very likely to result and his endeavours would be likely to add to the knowledge in a meaningful way.

A critical review of the literature enables the researcher to go into greater details and wider applicability of the problem in hand, so as to provide new ideas, explanations and hypotheses. The review forms an important chapter in a thesis where its purpose is to provide the background and justification for the research undertaken (Bruce, 1994) Bruce, who has identified six elements of a literature review. These elements comprise a list, a search; a report. A crucial element of all research degrees is the review of the relevant literature and its omission represents a void or absence of a major element in research.

Finally we can say that literature reviewed is to expand upon the context and to provide an empirical basis for the subsequent hypothesis. Study of related literature places the researcher in a better position to interpret the significance of his own results. The final and specific reason for reviewing related literature is to know the recommendations of the previous researchers for further research which they have listed in their studies. The length of the review will depend upon the number of relevant articles and the purpose for which the research report is being written. Literature review is not supposed to be just s summary of other people's work. Keeping their criteria in mind in the present investigations, the investigator surveyed a number of studies which are directly related to the present investigations and the same are reported here.

Review of the related literature helps the researchers to acquaint himself with current knowledge in the field or area in which researcher is going to conduct his research. The review of the related literature enables the researcher to define the limits of his fields and accordingly delimits or defines his problem.

The comparative study between private schools and government school conducted by Sharma K.J. (2008) in Bishnah zone of Jammu district, he found that private school teachers are specialists in subject teaching in only one or two subjects whereas government teachers are teaching all the subjects. From interviewing the parents, he came to know that parents of both private schools and government schools children think that private schools are better and therefore their first preference is the private schools. It also came to light that many factors are responsible for the decline in enrolment in government schools: Uneven distribution of teachers, transfer and delay in appointment, lack of dedication and commitment by the teachers, lack of accountability and supervision and poor performance of students in government school. He also found that mushrooming growth of private school is a contributing factor in the decline enrolment in government schools. He came up with a suggestion that government schools should open nursery and pre-primary sections to capture children below 6 years of age.

Zothanmawii (2007) took up a study on the functioning of Government and private Higher Secondary Schools in Aizawal, Mizoram, found that the numbers of students are more in government higher secondary schools since screening of students is not conducted. Private schools admitted a student on the basis of merit; hence, students are having good academic background. Government schools provided more facilities to students. Space provided for per child in private school is larger than in government school. Teachers in government schools are more experienced than their counterparts of private schools. Most of the private schools provided field trip to their students; a few government schools also provided field trip to students. Due to overcrowded class room, government school faced problems. Government school are more democratic in functioning. Private school principals performed more regular supervision of academic activities.

Kingdon G.G, (2007) examines that primary school participation rate improved in the early 1990'S (ASER 2006). But there was no change in secondary enrolment ratio. According to author, school participation depends on both the extent of demand for and the availability of supply of schooling, but there are only 1/5th as many secondary schools as the number of the primary schools. There was a great inter-state variation in gender disparity in case of secondary school enrolment rates. Using the gender disparity index for secondary school enrolment, the author found that higher gender inequality were in the States such as Bihar, Rajasthan than the other states while states like Kerala, Tamil Nadu, had attained gender parity. The major reason for this gender inequality in secondary enrolment was intra-household bias against women and household educational expenditure.

Mehar R, Dhillon and Sarkaria (2007) examines the performance differentials between male and female students in single sex and co-education schools of districts Amritsar and Gurdaspur of Punjab during academic sessions 1995-96 to 2001-02. To carry out this study a sample of nineteen schools was taken from rural, urban and semi-urban areas. The analysis based on observations revealed that female students outperformed their male counterpart in 11th and 12th classes of the three streams of study. They attributed differentials between male and female students in academic achievement to the socio-cultural variations of different type of habitations. In urban and semi-urban areas most of the parents are educated and daughters are less prone to gender disparity. Comparatively girls in rural areas have to devote more time to various domestic chores like cleaning, cooking and looking after their younger siblings. Further education of girls is not given as much importance as is given in urban and semi urban areas.

Chandra Kumar Singh (2006) conducted a comparative study of the government and private schools at Elementary Education in Imphal Municipal Block. He found that private schools come up in prosperous locations whereas government schools come up where there is demand from the public. Most of the government schools are functioning without the regular Head of the institution, this affect functioning of the schools. Head of the private institution enjoy more freedom in making plan for the development of their institution meanwhile the head of the government school have to go by the directives of the education officials. He also found out that private schools have comparatively better infrastructural facilities than the government. Teachers in private school are more motivated. The teachers in government schools are lacking in accountability due to political and bureaucratic intervention, teachers association and the socio-economic background of the students.

Shrivastva Ravi, (2005) examines the teacher availability at elementary level of education. She found that there were more than three teachers in urban areas in all school but there was single teacher school in rural areas. The proportion of single teacher school was low with the help of operation blackboard scheme. But still there was problem of the low availability of teachers. She estimated the percentage of filled and vacant teacher posts and reported that proportion of sanctioned teacher positions have remained unfilled. There was gender biasness for teacher appointments in rural area. She found the share of males & female teachers in school and more than two-third of teachers in rural primary schools were males and same situation seen in upper primary stage.

Govinda R. (2002) observes that wide inter- state disparities in enrolment in India. He found that in Madhya Pradesh (M.P), net enrolment ratio was high, which was 79.2%. But it was low in Bihar, Jammu and Kashmir (J&K), Nagaland, Rajasthan, Utter Pradesh (U.P) and West Bengal (W.B). However female enrolment ratio had shown a significant increase during the last few years. But there were gender disparities in some of the states like U.P., Rajasthan, J & K, and Bihar. The positive feature was reduction in dropout rate which was relatively sharper than that for the boys. This was the case due to the special attention paid to the girl's education over the recent years.

Sen Gupta and Guha, (2002) estimated the enrolment, dropout and grade completion of girl children in West Bengal. The study takes into consideration the girl children of age group 7 to 18 years. The author chose to focus on girls education as women in India tend to lag behind significantly both in comparison to their male counterparts as well as their sisters elsewhere in the world. The impact of parents educational level on child's education, income and occupation of parents etc. the study also observed, that working women, members of Muslim community, scheduled caste and scheduled tribe and rural residence has negative impact on education of children.

Singh Shailendra and Sridhar's study (2002) of two districts namely, Deoria & Firozabad in U.P. This study covered 54 government and 48 private schools. They found the decline in government school's enrolment and a commensurate increase of enrolment in private recognized school. The author focused on two time period i.e. 1997-98 to 1998-99 and 1998-99 to 1999-2000. In the case of gender, the higher number of girls were enrolled in government schools than the private schools, whereas is case of drop out; it was high in govt. schools than private school. In case of school infrastructure, the 94 government schools have their own buildings, own hand pumps, good classrooms, but this position was totally different in private schools. The Private schools have better health facility and electricity facility in schools. The teacher pupil ratio had increased over the period of time in private schools and their teachers were having better qualification. But in private schools, teachers are not trained because there are no training facilities for private school teachers. The study analyzed that comparative study between two districts through estimation of out of school children in private schools, enrolment rates using primary data.

One way of eliminating this selection bias is to randomly assign children to public and private schools and compare their learning outcomes. However, even well designed experiments do not always yield clear cut estimates of school effects. Voucher experiments in Colombia and Chile provide interesting examples. Colombia began experimenting with school vouchers in 1991 and provided vouchers to students entering grade 6 by randomly assigned lottery. This allows for a comparison of lottery winners and losers and the comparison indicates that the winners have lower dropout rate and somewhat higher tests scores than losers (Angrist et al. 2002).

Nautiyal (2001) studied the socio-economic problems in enrolment and retention of Muslim girls in the Haridwar district of Uttaranchal. He concluded that socio-economic background of the Muslim girls' parents was the primary cause of low enrolment & retention of Muslim girls.

A comparative study of the functioning of government and private schools of the Faridkot district, Punjab by Brar, S.K. (1998) finds out that majority of parents send their children to private schools because they feel that teachers are more dedicated, giving more care and attention to children. Private schools are more disciplined, efficient in administration, better in providing facilities to children, better in teaching and methods of evaluation. Highest percentage of teachers feel that quality of government schools is low compared to private schools due to transfer of teachers and delay in appointment, poor family background of students, excessive influence of political parties, engagement of teachers in census, election and other duties including clerical work in school and lack of school community relationship etc. Majority of government school headmasters reported that the quality of government school is low and the reason being lack of infrastructure, students poor family background, influence of strike, wastage of teachers time in census, election and other duties, lack of dedication and responsibility. On the other hand, majority of private schools headmasters reported that they attracted students to private schools because of the public feeling that better education is imparted, better infrastructure facilities more discipline and better coaching, more compulsory in teaching and learning, more incentives etc.

Singh, Suman K and KumarSunil, (1999) conducted a comparison of government and private schools in the rural areas of Muzzafarpur and Darbhanga district in Bihar. They found that most of the private schools had poor quality physical infrastructure, but better pre-primary teaching facilities that were nearly absent in the government schools. Government schools were found to have fewer, but well-trained teachers, although learning achievement was found to be higher in private than in government schools. Private school teachers worked harder and refrained from going on leave, which was not the case with government school teachers. A comparison of the profile of parents showed that preference for private schools was linked to their educational status and inspiration.

Probe Team, (1999) the report gives a recent picture of education system in India. It is the people's report which means that it puts forward the viewpoints of the common people regarding various issues related with education. The issue includes how important education is for boys and girls, the condition of schools, availability of teachers and school environment. The study area chosen here is Bihar, Madhya Pradesh, Rajasthan, and Uttar Pradesh. How much importance parents give to education in life, what they felt about sending their children to school, what is the cause behind withdrawing their children are some such questions the report has successfully tried to capture. All these issues have been taken up by the report. Broadly, the report includes issues like, accessibility of schools both physical and social along with economic accessibility, quality of infrastructure present in various government and private schools, school environment, cause of dropout, facts about teacher's involvement and community participation. It was found that maximum percentage of people felt that even the factors like, poor condition of schools, inadequate infrastructural facilities, unhealthy school environment and lack of teacher's commitment are responsible for the poor attendance and high dropout rates.

Duraismay (1999) studied cost, quality and outcomes of primary schooling in rural Tamil Nadu and came to the conclusion that the institutional cost of schooling was highest in the aided schools. The teachers in government schools were more educated and experienced. Students of private schools performed far better than students of government and government aided schools. Teachers' qualification, literacy of the pupils', father, student-teacher ratio in the class and type of school management exerted significant influence on the achievement of students.

Malhotra Sudha,(1998) based on a study of schools in Allahabad District in Uttar Pradesh found that while enrolment in schools giving incentives to students was higher than those that were not providing incentives. Attendance in schools without incentives was higher than those with incentives. The retention rate was higher in schools without incentives than their counterparts.

Singh Y.P, (1998) estimates the comparative analysis of government & private schools in Gorakhpur and Saharanpur districts in U.P. The author analyzed that the enrolment ratio was higher in government schools than private schools. The regular homework were given to the students in private schools that was found to be absent in government schools. The teachers give more attention to the students in private schools.

Aggarwal, Yash, (1998) study based on Delhi finds that teachers in private unaided schools (PUA) were younger and more qualified. It was easy for private unaided schools to appoint a teacher. But teacher appointment was a long procedure in govt. school. Because private unaided schools were not obliged to follow guidelines such as SC/ST reservation or seniority. He also estimated that govt. schools did not have good infrastructure but even 14 of the 40 private unaided schools did not have the toilets for girls.

Kiran Bhatty (1998) also focuses on the social prejudices and infrastructural bottlenecks that have impact on parental motivation with regard to education, she further points out that parents tried to favour education of male children while ignoring the educational needs of girls. This unequal favour from the parents' side leads to gender biasness. The author has included economic and social considerations in explaining gender biasness seen in the educational system in India. Factors such as, low economic and low social returns, tradition to early marriage and presence of higher levels of schools at a distance from the household etc force the parents to take out their girl children from schools. The author, while enumerating the role of the above mentioned factors, attempts to establish that low parental motivation is not a cause of poor enrolment and high drop out of children in elementary classes.

Babukuttan P. (1997) in his study on existing inspection and supervision of primary schools in Kollam district, Kerala, also finds lack of physical facilities, lack of awareness regarding new concepts of supervision as the common problems faced by inspecting officers. He showed that office works consume most of their time.

Hailu (1997) in Eritrea have revealed that number of female teachers has a strong bearing on the participation of girls. The authors report that low percentage of girls (28%) in secondary school is because percentage of female teachers is very low (9%).

Kingdom, Geeta, Gandhi, (1996) points out towards a crucial distinction namely the difference between "recognized" and "unrecognized" private unaided schools. State government recognition is an official stamp of approval but it requires certain conditions to be fulfilled. While all private unaided secondary schools must be recognized, elementary schools do not have to be recognized in many states. The main reason for wanting recognition is to become eligible to apply for government grant-in-aid and to be able to issue valid Transfer certificates to students leaving the school.

Duraisamy (1996) finds that education level of private unaided schools teachers were not very different from those private aided schools. But the number of experience years was less in private unaided schools as compared to government and aided schools. On the other side; the government and private aided schools spend less on school infrastructure as compared to private unaided schools because teacher's salaries were less in private unaided schools as compared to government and private unaided schools.

Tamjenkaba, (1993) reported that: (i) Christian Missionaries played an important role to establish schools in the then Naga Hills. Dr. and Mrs. Clark started the first School at Moleng Ymsim in 1878 with the enrolments of 6 students. After the 2nd World War, more people got interested to receive education. (ii) Development of Education in Nagaland started after the attainment of statehood of Nagaland while participating in the National Five Years Plans, starting from the Fourth Five Year Plan.

Solanki K.N., (1992) conducted a study on the relationship between the educational management and the organisational climate. The finding revealed that (1) education management of a school depended upon the resources of the school system. It was independent of sex of student's population, of organisational management and place of school but mostly depended upon the human educational and physical dimensions of resources, (2) the Secondary Schools differed among themselves in their organisational climate. The organisational level of Secondary School appeared to be independent of organisational management, place of work and sex of student's population, (3) there was a relationship between a resource management system and the organisational climate of the school. Highly resourceful were inclined towards the open range climate, whereas the low resourceful schools were inclined towards the closed ranged climate.

On the contribution of Seng Khasi schools to the development of education in Meghalaya, Talang D.H., (1992) found that Seng Khasi School is the only sectarian secular private educational institution in the state of Meghalaya. The aim of the school is to propagate education and traditional institution to all section of the people in the society. The school was founded in the year 1921 and was recognised by the government in 1964. Administration of the school was carried out by the headmaster with the help of teachers along with the managing committee. Annual grant to the school was borne by the state government. The school provides a library for the students where magazines, journals and reference books on different subjects are kept.

Pati S., (1992) revealed that in Cuttack-I circle, Cuttack, a majority of the Secondary School Headmaster did not have adequate provision for audio-visual aids in their school. In majority of schools, various activities like sports etc. existed but they did not have funds for organising co-curricular activities in their schools. All the headmasters stated that their colleagues assisted them in their office work. In some schools only there were a required number of peons and majority of them did not have a typing machine.

A study by Morgan V., (1992) focuses on the question of how to interact schools in Northern Ireland. It suggests that the role of the head teacher makes increased demands on the person in such schools. It also suggests that the group of head teachers is to some extent be self selective to take up the position requires a deep commitment to the ideals of integrated education. The three key areas where their experiences are emphasized are curricular development and implementation, management skills and relationship with parents.

Birdi B. (1992) in his study highlights the fact that the work of inspecting officer has increased without any corresponding increase in the strength of staff. The study has another interesting observation to make regarding the methods and procedures of supervision and inspection: it has not undergone much change since independence.

In the Darrang District of Assam, Deka B.N., (1991) found that the increases in population, poverty of the people, illiteracy of the parents, indifferent attitude towards female education, inadequate financial resources have contributed to the backwardness of the Secondary Education in the District. The socio-economic condition of teachers is far from satisfactory. The private school teachers particularly get lower scale of pay with insecurities of service. Under such conditions no such teachers can be expected to discharge his duties with credibility and sincerity. He also points out the problems such as: inadequate school infrastructures, less number of trained teachers, lack of co-curricular activities and neglected physical education and lack of understanding between parents and teachers. Proper supervision and inspection of the school is absent especially in remote and backward areas. Teacher's condition and status were neglected by the government, political leaders and the public. No introduction of subjects which suited to the local needs, e.g., crafts and SUPW was made and financial hardship is the root of all evils in the field of Secondary Education in Darrang District.

CHAPTER – III
RESEARCH METHODOLOGY AND PROCEDURE

Introduction

The common idea of methodology is the collection, the comparative study and critique of the individual method that is used in a given discipline or field of inquiry. It can be defined as (i) a body of method, rules and postulates employed by a discipline. (ii) A particular procedure or set of procedures. (iii) The analysis of the principles of procedures of inquiry in a particular field. Research, being a methodological approach, is a vast and multi-dimensional concept. It is an endless quest for knowledge or an unending search for truth. It brings to light new knowledge, corrects previous errors and miss-conceptions and adds an orderly way to the existing body of knowledge .The knowledge obtained by search is scientific and objective. Therefore it is implied that for obtaining scientific and objective results, there should be a proper methodology and procedure.

Every piece of research must be planned and designed carefully so that the researcher proceeds ahead without getting confused at the subsequent steps of research. The researcher must have a clean and clear understanding of what is to be done, what data is needed, what data collecting tools are to be employed and how the data is to be statistically analyzed and interpreted?

A design is a blueprint of the procedure for the completion of various research steps and thus reaching valid conclusions regarding the relationship between the variables under study. Therefore, it is important that the design is specifically conceived and objectively executed to bring empirical evidence. By doing so, the observations and inferences become valid to rely on. The preparation of a research proposal or design is an important step in the research process. It provides a systematic plan and procedure for the research to follow.

"Research design sets up the framework for adequate tests of the relations among variables. Design tells us, in the sense, what observation to make, how to make them and how to analyses the quantitative representation of the observations. Strictly speaking, design doesn't tell us precisely what to do, but rather suggests the direction of the observation making and analysis" (Kerlinger1983, p.27)

Research design stands for advance planning of the method to be adopted for collecting the relevant data and the techniques to be used in their analysis. Selection of a particular design is based on the purpose of the piece of research to be conducted. The design deals with selection of the subjects, selection of the data gathering devices, the procedure of making observations and the type of statistical analysis to be employed in interpreting data relationship.

A research study is to be carried out as per a design formulated in anticipation. The present study is based on survey method. The present investigator also formulated a compact design to carry out the research. The details about the sample, tools employed, scoring, data collection, procedure and analysis are given as under:

Research Design

The study should be viewed as exploratory in nature. The methods adopted for the present study is a combination of exploration and description. The exploratory design was selected because of the fulfillment of research needs as per the objectives. Although in India there are a few researches conducted on development of education. Various new approaches have adopted to find out the research queries. Further the nature of research is descriptive as well because it contains some assumed findings.

Data Base

Information was gathered by using a variety of methods to gain a better understanding of the situation, issues, perspectives and priorities. Data collections methods were included documents/literature review, structured interviews and questionnaires. The data regarding different parameters of the study was collected from different institutes of education and training in four districts of South Kashmir viz; Anantnag, Pulwama, Shopian and Kulgam. The investigator also collected the data from State Board of School Education, Srinagar, different District Institutes of education and Training, different Census Hand Books of

Government of Jammu and Kashmir and different surveys and studies about the growth and development of education in South Kashmir.

In the present study the primary as well as secondary sources of data was utilized to obtain the information.

Primary Data

Primary data was collected in almost all the educational zones, colleges etc with the use of designed information blank, questionnaire and structured interview schedule. The information blank was collected from different educational offices and educational zones of South Kashmir. The questionnaire was conducted individually asking by headmasters of different public and private institutions of South Kashmir, Jammu and Kashmir, besides that questionnaire was also administered to the parents whose children are enrolled in public and private institutions. An interview was conducted on different teachers who are engaged in teaching in different public and private institutions of South Kashmir. An interview was also conducted to different educationists (Director School education, Joint Director School Education, Chief Education Officers and Zonal Education Officers of South Kashmir).

Secondary Data

Secondary data was collected from various books, journals, newspapers, magazines and other relevant sources. Websites which contain lot of material on educational development of India as well as Kashmir. Besides that secondary data was also collected from the Chief Education Offices and Zonal Education Offices, Digest of Statistics, Directorate of Economics and Statistics, Government of Jammu and Kashmir and Census Hand Books of J&K.

Sample for the Present Study

The investigator collected the data from different educational and learning institutions of South Kashmir. The list of data collected for the present study was as under:

1. Jammu and Kashmir State Board of School Education, Bemina, Srinagar.
2. Directorate of Economics and Statistics, Government of Jammu and Kashmir, Bemina, Srinagar.
3. Old Secretariat, Government of Jammu and Kashmir, Jahangir Chock, Srinagar.
4. District Institutes of Education and Training, Anantnag, Kashmir.
5. District Institutes of Education and Training, Pulwama, Kashmir.
6. District Institutes of Education and Training, Kulgam, Kashmir.
7. District Institutes of Education and Training, Shopian, Kashmir.
8. Chief Education Office, Anantnag, Kashmir.
9. Chief Education Office, Pulwama, Kashmir.
10. Chief Education Office, Kulgam, Kashmir.
11. Chief Education Office, Shopian, Kashmir.

Tools and Techniques

The data for the present study was collected through information blank, questionnaire for headmasters and parents and interview schedule for educationists. Following tools and techniques were employed for the present investigation:

1. Information blank – I
2. Information blank – II
3. Information blank – III
4. Questionnaire – I (For headmasters)
5. Questionnaire – II (For parents)
6. Questionnaire – III (For teachers)
7. Interview schedule (For educationists)

CHAPTER – IV
ANALYSIS AND INTERPRETATION OF THE DATA

Profile of Kashmir

J&K State Profile: Kashmir has remained a land of Sufis, Rishis and Saints and above all, cultured people. The culture of the state is a product of a great and continuous interaction between Hindus, Muslims and Sikhs. The state of Jammu and Kashmir enjoys a special status in the country. It has its own constitution which regulates its ways for socio-economic development of its people. The state has a unique feature of having two capitals, Jammu as the winter capital for 6 months (November-April) and Srinagar as the summer capital for 6 months (May-October).

Situated between 32.15 degree and 37.05 degree north latitude and 72.35 degree and 83.20degree east longitude, the total area of the state is 2, 22,236 sq. kms. including 78,114 sq. kms under the illegal occupation of Pakistan and 37,555 sq.kms under that of China, of which Pakistan illegally handed over 5,180 sq kms. to China. The length of the state is 640 kms. From north–south and 480 kms from east–west.

The state of Jammu and Kashmir is situated in the extreme north of India. It is bounded by China in the north and east, by Afghanistan in the north-west and by Pakistan in the west. In the south it has its boundaries with the states of Punjab and Himachal Pradesh. The state commands a strategic importance in Asia due to its central location.

Geographically and culturally, the state has three main regions: Jammu, Kashmir and Ladakh. The annual rainfall also varies from region to region with 115.9mm, 650.5mm and 92.6mm respectively. The state of Jammu and Kashmir which is an abode of love, beauty and location, makes it undoubtedly the crown of India. The largest fresh water lake in the Asia namely "Wular Lake" is also located in Kashmir.

The state ranks 6th in area and 19th in population among the state and union territories of India. Now the state has 22 revenue districts as 8 new districts have been created on 1st

April, 2007out of which Leh and Kargil fall in the cold arid zone. The districts of Srinagar, Baramulla, Kupwara, Bandipura, Ganderbal, Pulwama, Budgam, Shopian, Kulgam and Anantnag are located in the temperate zone of Kashmir valley which remains snow-bound during winter. The districts of Jammu, Punch, Rajouri, Kathua, Kishtwar, Ramban, Reasi, Samba, Udhampur and Doda fall in the sub-tropical zone. The state has 142 blocks, 74tehsils, 3 municipalities and 6758 villages. The state is connected with rest of the country by air, rail and road. Air India and other private airlines operate regular flights to Srinagar, Jammu and Leh.

The national highway 1-A connects the capital cities of Srinagar and Jammu with rest of the country. There are daily passenger trains connecting Jammu with most of the major cities of the country. The state consists of mostly mountains with a large area of forests. Agriculture is the main occupation of the people. Paddy, wheat and maize are the major crops. The area also offers good climatic conditions for the cultivation of fresh and dry fruits. Paper mashie, wood carving, carpets, shawl-making, embroidery etc., are among Kashmir's exquisite handicrafts which earn substantial foreign exchange. Official language is Urdu but English is mostly used in the offices. Kashmiri, Boshi, Dogri and Pahari are the mother tongues in different regions.

The population of the state is 1, 25, 48,956 of which 66, 65,561are males and 58,83,365 are females according to the census of 2011.The state has literacy rate of 68.74% as per the census of 2011 with 78.26% male literates and 58.01% female literates. The density of the state is 124 persons per sq.kms.

Educational Statistics: At present there are 28824 schools in the state of Jammu and Kashmir of which15245 are primary schools, 10008 are middle schools and 3519 are secondary/higher secondary schools. Besides these there are 2 sainik schools, 36 kendriya vidyalayas and 14 jawahar navodaya vidyalaya's, army good will schools, kasburba gandhi balika vidyalaya's, darul-ulooms which also impart education to the children.

Higher Education: Besides primary, upper primary and secondary educational institutions in the state of Jammu and Kashmir, there are also various colleges of higher learning which are disseminating knowledge in the state. Among them there are 95 colleges for general education, 142 B. ed colleges, 3 medical colleges, 4 engineering colleges, 53 industrial training institutes, 30 polytechnic colleges, 7 nursing colleges, paramedical institutes and other professional and non-professional colleges. There are 8 universities in the state of Jammu and Kashmir of which 2 are central universities, 1 is a technical university, 1 is an agricultural university and 4 are state universities. Among the state universities, the University of Jammu and the University of Kashmir have their campuses in various districts of Jammu and Kashmir.

Profile of South Kashmir: South Kashmir region is situated 15 km south-east of Srinagar. The population is 23, 28,950 of which 12, 03,366 are males and 11, 25,584 are females as per the census of 2011. South Kashmir is called the gateway of Kashmir valley. The area is bounded by Srinagar in the north, Rajori in the north-west and Kargil district in the north-east and also bounded by Doda and Udhampur in the east and south. The area is bounded by pir-panjal mountain range through which passes the world famous Jawahar Tunnel. Also due to the trees lining up all along the roads in this area it is called the 'green tunnel' of the valley. This area is connected to the rest of India by road and rail links. The only national highway which passes through the state of Jammu and Kashmir passes through this region.

So far as the agriculture is concerned, the area is very fertile. This area is also called the green belt of Kashmir valley. About 51% of the total area is covered with forest and 82% population lives in the villages. Most of the population is engaged in agriculture. Because of the good fertility of soil and high production of rice, the area is also called the "rice bowl of Kashmir". The area is also famous all over the world for the saffron cultivation, production of walnut and apple. Most of the higher reaches of South Kashmir experience early snowfall in winters. This area is also known for its high and quality production of milk in the valley.

South Kashmir has been divided into two districts in 1979 namely Anantnag and Pulwama. In 2007, these districts were further divided and the district of Anantnag gave birth to Kulgam and the district of Pulwama gave birth to Shopian. Kashmiri and Urdu are the main languages of people while rice is their staple food.

The area of the South Kashmir also gained significance during the Muslim period when Aurangzeb's governor Islam Khan (1664-65) laid out a garden for the Mughal Emperor who named the place after him as "Islamabad". The dogra ruler Gulab Singh however rechristened the town as 'Anantnag'.

Tourist Attractions: South Kashmir attracts people not only from within India but from the whole world because the area is full of attractions which are globally famous like Pahalgam, Achabal, Kokernag, Verinag, Simthantop, Aharbal waterfall, Awanti Varman Monuments in Awantipora etc., The famous river Jhelum also originates from South Kashmir region.

As far as the education sector of the South Kashmir region is concerned, there are a large number of private and public schools which cater to the education of children up to the higher secondary level. There is a campus of the University of Kashmir in the district of Anantnag and also a technical university namely the Islamic University of Science and Technology in Awantipora in district of Pulwama. Besides these, there are a large number of professional and non professional colleges/institutes which cater to the higher education in this region. The statistics related to these institutions and schools have been discussed in detail in the following pages which will help us get an accurate picture of the educational sector in the South Kashmir region.

Notwithstanding the precision of data computation, an investigator needs to be equally critical and selective in choosing an appropriate statistical method for the analysis of data. Because an inadequate statistical analysis will make the whole process a meaningless collection of tables and figures. It is pertinent to understand the objectives under investigation and then employ a suitable statistical device so as to differentiate between the known variables and factors which interfere with their performance.

SECTION – A
PRIVATE AND PUBLIC INSTITUTIONS ENGAGED IN DISSEMINATING
KNOWLEDGE IN SOUTH KASHMIR

India as a country came into existence in the year 1947, so our study primarily focuses on the changes which have taken place in the education system in the area of South Kashmir after India has attained independence. In doing so we have collected the data from 1948-2013. A general overview of the system in existence at the time of our independence can be obtained from the data which we have included from the year 1948. The data which was obtained for the period 1951-2011 was on the basis of changes which took place decade wise which gives us an accurate picture of the changes which have taken place during these 10 years. After 2011, the data from the years 2012 and 2013 has also been included to provide additional reference for obtaining a clear and latest picture of how the system works today. In some tables it may be noticed that the data is not from the starting period of our study but starts from an intermediate period like 1981 or 2011. The reason for omitting the periods which are not mentioned in the table is given as a small explanation which is annexed to each table.

Table No. 4.1: Showing the total number of primary schools in South Kashmir from 1948 to 2013

Year	Public/ Private	Total number of schools	Total enrolment	Male	Female	Total number of teachers	Male	Female	Pupil teacher ratio
1948	Public	160	4812	4600	212	412	412	0	12:1
	Private	13	902	881	21	27	27	0	13:1
1951	Public	323	11430	10914	516	696	696	0	16:1
	Private	26	2200	2161	39	48	48	0	46:1
1961	Public	516	17690	16967	723	1471	1440	31	12:1
	Private	37	4110	3283	827	93	93	0	44:1
1971	Public	695	23220	22007	1213	1530	1410	120	15:1
	Private	41	4888	3328	1560	158	129	29	31:1
1981	Public	908	42633	32977	9656	2628	2297	331	16:1
	Private	62	8422	5022	3400	296	249	47	28:1
1991	Public	1048	57044	40323	16721	3085	2685	400	18:1
	Private	82	12302	5781	6521	534	441	93	23:1
2001	Public	1100	55047	33957	21090	4188	3069	1119	13:1
	Private	108	16852	9197	6755	728	455	273	23:1
2011	Public	1816	82229	46613	35616	7013	4738	2275	12:1
	Private	222	41025	21698	19327	1570	936	634	26:1
2012	Public	1800	83353	45685	37668	7151	4847	2304	12:1
	Private	229	43545	22716	20829	1629	887	742	27:1
2013	Public	1793	82836	45444	37392	7188	4865	2323	12:1
	Private	231	43917	23138	20779	1700	950	750	26:1

Source: Field Survey

The table 4.1 shows the statistics about the primary schools both private and public in the South Kashmir region. We can see a large increase in the enrolment in the schools and also the number of schools has increased dramatically. The main point which needs to be seen is the male female ratio among the students in the schools which has improved considerably. This shows a growing interest among the public to educate the girl child and also improved emphasis on the education of children.

Table No. 4.2: **Showing the total number of upper primary schools in South Kashmir from 1948 to 2013**

Year	Public/ Private	Upper primary schools							
		Total number of schools	Total enrolment	Male	Female	Total number of teachers	Male	Female	Pupil teacher ratio
1948	Public	66	5430	5213	217	330	330	0	16:1
	Private	4	452	440	12	38	38	0	12:1
1951	Public	93	7660	7141	519	412	412	0	19:1
	Private	7	1108	1069	39	63	63	0	18:1
1961	Public	161	18612	16863	1749	570	498	72	33:1
	Private	7	1203	1142	61	66	66	0	18:1
1971	Public	192	26825	24464	2361	911	790	121	29:1
	Private	9	1801	1685	116	91	84	7	20:1
1981	Public	288	34991	26864	8127	1684	1471	213	21:1
	Private	52	8312	6497	1815	459	395	64	18:1
1991	Public	330	45056	33845	11211	2362	1953	409	19:1
	Private	80	13280	8938	4342	638	530	108	21:1
2001	Public	640	50764	30029	20735	3726	2820	906	14:1
	Private	140	28971	16287	12684	998	862	136	29:1
2011	Public	1133	66626	35217	31409	6543	4848	1695	10:1
	Private	276	47766	24408	23358	2094	1548	546	23:1
2012	Public	1138	62314	32591	29723	6578	4869	1709	12:1
	Private	290	50522	27244	23778	2164	1597	567	27:1
2013	Public	1140	60297	31277	29020	6611	4873	1738	12:1
	Private	295	51537	26330	25207	2216	1622	594	26:1

Source: Field Survey

The above table shows the statistics about the upper primary schools both private and public in the South Kashmir region. We can see a large increase in the enrolment in the schools and also the no of schools has increased dramatically. The main point which needs to be seen is the male female ratio among the students in the schools which has improved considerably. This shows a growing interest among the public to educate the girl child and also improved emphasis on the education of children.

Table No. 4.3: **Showing the total number of secondary schools in South Kashmir from 1948 to 2013**

Year	Public/ Private	Secondary Schools							
		Total number of schools	Total enrolment	Male	Female	Total number of teachers	Male	Female	Pupil teacher ratio
1948	Public	20	3030	2964	66	145	145	0	21:1
	Private	2	228	203	25	19	25	0	12:1
1951	Public	27	5500	5311	189	243	243	0	23:1
	Private	2	220	201	19	20	81	0	11:1
1961	Public	36	7300	6980	320	420	403	17	17:1
	Private	02	238	211	27	21	101	0	11:1
1971	Public	40	10700	9645	1055	525	484	41	20:1
	Private	04	815	670	45	41	137	0	20:1
1981	Public	45	12380	9748	2632	615	533	82	20:1
	Private	13	3311	2492	819	188	161	27	18:1
1991	Public	88	22922	18036	4886	936	759	177	24:1
	Private	33	7913	4856	3057	398	304	94	20:1
2001	Public	124	23983	15586	8397	1581	1212	369	15:1
	Private	51	15089	8863	6226	623	488	135	24:1
2011	Public	217	48260	26870	21390	2825	1925	900	17:1
	Private	101	30487	15736	14751	1206	907	299	25:1
2012	Public	233	49889	27252	22637	2929	2002	927	17:1
	Private	107	32884	16489	16395	1255	946	309	26:1
2013	Public	233	49278	27028	22250	3008	2053	955	16:1
	Private	108	33528	17353	16175	1281	948	333	26:1

Source: Field Survey

The table 4.19 shows the statistics about the secondary schools both private and public in the South Kashmir Region. We can see a large increase in the enrolment in the schools and also the no of schools has increased dramatically. The main point which needs to be seen is the male female ratio among the students in the schools which has improved considerably. This shows a growing interest among the public to educate the girl child and also improved emphasis on the education of children. Also we can notice that the enrolment in the private secondary schools is increasing on a much faster pace compared to the public Schools.

Table No. 4.4: **Showing the total number of higher secondary schools in South Kashmir from 1948 to 2013**

Year	Public/ Private	Total number of schools	Total enrolment	Male	Female	Total number of teachers	Male	Female	Pupil teacher ratio
					Higher secondary schools				
1948	Public	3	684	667	17	27	27	0	25:1
	Private	0	0	0	0	0	0	0	0:1
1951	Public	3	704	613	91	31	31	0	23:1
	Private	0	0	0	0	0	0	0	0:1
1961	Public	5	856	760	96	75	75	0	11:1
	Private	0	0	0	0	0	0	0	0:1
1971	Public	12	2201	2079	122	137	123	14	16:1
	Private	1	260	221	39	12	12	0	22:1
1981	Public	13	4247	3713	534	288	256	32	15:1
	Private	1	280	217	63	13	13	0	22:1
1991	Public	27	8344	7189	1155	504	441	63	17:1
	Private	5	1080	789	291	58	51	7	19:1
2001	Public	50	21582	12734	8848	783	622	161	28:1
	Private	11	2551	1757	794	151	125	26	17:1
2011	Public	85	44897	26962	17935	1748	1280	468	26:1
	Private	23	4739	2859	1883	265	210	55	18:1
2012	Public	85	46525	27389	19136	1817	1308	509	26:1
	Private	23	5097	2965	2132	278	209	69	18:1
2013	Public	88	47909	27739	20170	1861	1340	521	26:1
	Private	23	5561	3216	2345	291	214	77	19:1

Source: Field Survey

The above table shows the statistics about the higher secondary schools both private and public in the South Kashmir region. We can see a large increase in the enrolment in the schools and also the no of schools has increased dramatically. The main point which needs to be seen is the male female ratio among the students in the schools which has improved considerably. This shows a growing interest among the public to educate the girl child and also improved emphasis on the education of children. The peculiar feature here is that the public schools are still more popular than the private schools for the higher secondary education. The easy availability of private tuitions makes a lot of students uninterested in taking admission in the private schools.

Table No. 4.5: **Showing the total number of district institutes of education and trainings in South Kashmir from 1951-2013**

Year	Total number of DIET`s	Total number of teachers trained	Male	Female
1951	1	95	90	5
1961	3	385	373	12
1971	3	762	718	44
1981	4	1523	1414	109
1991	4	2290	2046	244
2001	4	3975	2890	1085
2011	4	6015	3978	2037
2012	4	6930	4654	2276
2013	4	7750	5419	2310

Source: Field Survey

The above table shows that the number of DIET's has increased from 1 in 1951 to 4 in 2013 in the same period the number of teachers trained has increased from 95 to 7750. The male to female ratio has also improved from 18:1 in 1951 to 2.34:1 in the year 2013.This shows that the females who are getting into this profession are increasing day by day.

Table No. 4.6: **Showing the total number of government degree colleges in South Kashmir from 1948-2013**

Year	Total number of colleges	Total number of enrolment	Male	Female	Total number of teachers	Male	Female
1951	1	86	80	6	8	8	0
1961	1	128	124	4	15	15	0
1971	1	347	321	26	28	28	0
1981	2	808	702	106	42	39	3
1991	5	2729	1745	984	99	80	19
2001	5	9229	5427	3802	204	140	64
2011	14	29133	16451	12682	528	386	142
2012	14	30063	16036	14027	567	404	163
2013	14	31286	16785	14501	627	458	169

Source: Field Survey

The above table shows that there has been an increase in the number of govt degree colleges from 1 in 1951 to 14 in 2013. There also has been a dramatic increase in the number of students enrolled in these colleges from 71 in 1948 to 31286 in 2013. We can also see that there has been a very good change in the male to female ratio in these colleges which was 12.5:1 in 1948 which improved to 1.15:1 in the year 2013. There has also been a change in the male to female ratio in the teachers, from having no female teachers in 1948-1971 we have a healthy ratio of 2.71:1 in the year 2013. This shows that there has been a lot of improvement in the female education sector.

Table No. 4.7: **Showing the total number of government nursing colleges in South Kashmir from 2001-2013**

Year	Total No. of Colleges	Total No. of Enrolment	Male	Female	Total No. of Teachers	Male	Female
2001	1	100	30	70	5	2	3
2011	1	200	40	160	6	1	5
2012	1	200	61	139	6	0	6
2013	1	300	121	179	7	0	7

Source: Field Survey

The above table shows the statistics about the Government Nursing colleges in South Kashmir. The first nursing college in the South Kashmir Region was established in 2001. The above table shows that there has been an increase of enrolment in the government nursing colleges from 100 in 2001 to 300 in 2013.

Table No. 4.8: **Showing the total number of private paramedical institutes in South Kashmir from 2011-2013**

Year	Total number of institutes	Total number of enrolment	Male	Female	Total number of teachers	Male	Female
2011	7	577	202	375	65	34	31
2012	7	620	239	381	60	25	35
2013	7	801	375	426	99	54	45

Source: Field Survey

The above table shows the statistics about the private paramedical institutes in South Kashmir region. The first private paramedical institute was established in the decade 2001-2011. The table shows that there has been an increase in the enrolment in the private paramedical institutes from 577 in 2011 to 801 in 2013.

Table No. 4.9:   Showing the total number of Kasturba Gandhi Balika Vidyalaya schools in South Kashmir from 2011-2013

Year	Total number of schools	Total number of enrolment	Male	Female	Total number of teachers	Male	Female
2011	4	200	0	200	19	1	18
2012	4	200	0	200	23	0	23
2013	4	200	0	200	20	0	20

Source: Field Survey

The above table shows the statistics about the Kasturba Gandhi Balika Vidyalaya in the South Kashmir region. The fist school was established in the decade 2001-2011. This table shows no change in the enrolment as this is a part of a central govt scheme which is intended for providing education to a fixed number of female children who fall under.

Table No. 4.10: Showing the total number of industrial training institutes in South Kashmir from 1981-2013

Year	Total number of institutes	Total number of enrolment	Male	Female	Total number of teachers	Male	Female
1981	1	80	44	36	7	6	1
1991	3	290	190	100	17	15	2
2001	3	362	241	121	27	22	5
2011	5	1336	891	445	70	56	14
2012	5	1699	1143	556	74	60	14
2013	5	1789	1195	594	76	60	16

Source: Field Survey

The table shows the statistics about the industrial training institutes in the south Kashmir region. The industrial training institute which was in existence before 1981 was badly damaged in a fire accident and the institute was re-established in the year 1981. The above

40

table shows that there has been an increase in the total number of institutes from 1 in 1981 to 5 in 2013, the enrolment in these institutes has also increased from 0 in 1981 to 1789 in 2013. The male to female ratio has decreased from 1.22:1 in 1981 to 2.01: 1 in 2013. This shows a decreasing interest in the female community in these types of courses.

Table No. 4.11: Showing the total number of kendriya vidyalaya schools in South Kashmir from 2011-2013

Year	Total number of schools	Total number of enrolment	Male	Female	Total number of teachers	Male	Female
2011	3	328	228	100	24	17	7
2012	3	343	262	81	21	16	5
2013	3	296	215	81	24	16	8

Source: Field Survey

The above table shows the statistics about the kendriya vidyalaya schools in the South Kashmir region. The first kendriya vidyalaya School was opened in the decade 2001-2011. The above shows that there has been a marginal increase in the number of students enrolled from 2011 to 2012, but there has been a decrease afterwards with the number of students falling to 296 in the year 2013. This has been because in this time there has been a dramatic increase in the number of private schools and the parent's interest in sending their children to these schools has decreased.

Table No. 4.12: Showing the total number of government polytechnic colleges in South Kashmir from 2012-2013

Year	Total number of colleges	Total number of enrolment	Male	Female	Total number of teachers	Male	Female
2012	4	394	292	102	37	33	4
2013	4	750	512	238	49	42	7

Source: Field Survey

The above table shows the statistics about the government polytechnic colleges in South Kashmir region. The first polytechnic college was established in the year 2012. The table shows the number of students enrolled in the government polytechnic colleges has increased from 394 in 2012 to 750 in 2013. These colleges have been started in the year 2012 only and there were no government polytechnic colleges in South Kashmir before.

Table No. 4.13: Showing the total number of Jawahar Novodaya Vidyalaya schools in South Kashmir from 1991-2013

Year	Total number of schools	Total number of enrolment	Male	Female	Total number of teachers	Male	Female
1991	1	80	52	28	15	15	-
2001	2	370	260	110	37	28	9
2011	2	394	258	136	40	31	9
2012	2	508	342	156	41	29	12
2013	2	496	335	161	42	29	13

Source: Field Survey

The above table shows the statistics about the jawahar novodaya vidyalaysas in the South Kashmir region. The first jawahar navodaya vidyalayas in India were established in the year 1986 and the first school in this region has been established in the year 1988. The above table shows that there has been an increase of enrolment in the jawahar navodaya vidyalaya schools from 1991 to 2012 but there has been a marginal decrease in number in the year 2013. This decrease can be attributed to parents losing interest in sending their wards to these fully residential schools and also mushrooming of private schools at the same time.

Table No. 4.14: Showing the total number of army goodwill schools in South Kashmir from 2001-2013

Year	Total number of schools	Total number of enrolment	Male	Female	Total number of teachers	Male	Female
2001	2	448	239	209	20	14	6
2011	4	1370	900	470	69	46	23
2012	4	1446	901	545	74	47	27
2013	4	1529	961	568	76	50	26

Source: Field Survey

The army goodwill schools in Jammu and Kashmir are schools setup and run by the Indian army in the far flung areas where there are very less number of private schools. These schools are intended for the benefit of general public. The first army goodwill school has been established in 2001. The above table shows that there has been an increase in the number of students enrolled in these schools, from 448 in 2001 to 1529 in 2013. This shows the growing interest among parents in sending their children to these schools as they provide a good quality of education which earlier not available to them.

Table No. 4.15: **Showing the total number of private college (academic) in South Kashmir from 1961-2013**

Year	Total number of schools	Total number of enrolment	Male	Female	Total number of teachers	Male	Female
1961	1	43	43	0	4	4	0
1971	1	108	108	0	7	7	0
1981	1	133	133	0	8	8	0
1991	1	252	252	0	14	14	0
2001	1	255	196	59	15	15	0
2011	1	300	230	70	15	12	3
2012	1	378	268	110	16	11	5
2013	1	431	236	193	18	11	7

Source: Field Survey

The first private academic college in the South Kashmir region was established in the year 1961. This is the only private college in the South Kashmir region till date. The institute has a special distinction of starting as a religious training institute in 1961 which later transformed into a proper academic college where today English, Urdu, Arabic, Islamic Studies and Computer Science are the subjects offered, besides these the college also offer 1-2 religious courses .The above table shows that there has been an increase in the enrolment of students in the lone private Academic College from 43 in 1961 and 431 in 2013. The male to female ratio in this college has also increased dramatically from having no female student in 1961 to having a ratio of 1.22:1 in 2013. This shows the growing interest among the girl students to have a good education.

Table No. 4.16: Showing the total number of darul-ulooms in South Kashmir from 1948-2013

Year	Total number of darul-ulooms	Total number of enrolment	Male	Female	Total number of teachers	Male	Female
1948	1	13	11	2	2	2	0
1951	1	78	66	12	11	11	0
1961	1	141	98	43	15	15	0
1971	1	183	147	36	19	19	0
1981	1	240	169	71	26	26	0
1991	2	433	304	129	44	44	0
2001	2	812	599	213	61	52	9
2011	2	1265	905	260	82	70	12
2012	2	1318	940	378	101	80	21
2013	2	1464	1063	401	103	80	23

Source: Field Survey

Darul-ulooms are educational institutions set up by religious trusts and provide both religious and general education at the same time. These institutions also provide residential facilities for its students. These institutions while also granting standard educational certificates, grant certificate for the study in religious education. The above table shows that there has been an increase in the number of students enrolled in these institutions from 13 in 1948 to 1063 in 2013. The male female ratio has also improved from 5.5:1 in 1948 to 2.65:1 in 2013. This also shows that there has been a continuing interest among the student community in pursuing religious education along with general education.

Table No. 4.17: Showing the total number of private professional colleges in South Kashmir from 1995-2013

Year	Total number of colleges	Total number of enrolment	Male	Female	Total number of teachers	Male	Female
1995	1	160	81	79	15	9	6
2001	1	185	99	86	15	9	6
2011	14	2957	1690	1267	174	103	71
2012	14	3098	1779	1319	183	105	78
2013	14	3254	1983	1271	191	112	79

Source: Field Survey

The above table shows the statistics about the private professional colleges in the South Kashmir region. The first private professional college was established in the year 1995. The above table shows that there has been an increase in the number of private professional colleges from 1 in 1995 to 14 in 2013 and there has been a dramatic increase in the number of students enrolled in these colleges from 160 in 1995 to 3254 in 2013. This shows the growing interest among the student community to develop skills required in the professional arena.

MAJOR FINDINGS OF THE ABOVE SECTION

While analysing the data of (private and public) schools in all four districts of South Kashmir, It was found that there is large increase in the enrolment and number of schools has increased dramatically. It was also found that students (male- female) ratio in the schools has improved considerably. This implies that there is growing interest among the public to educate the girl child and also improved emphasis on the education of children. It was found that the female education which was below 5% in 1948 is now almost equal. The investigator also found that female teachers have also increased dramatically. Data shows that there is substantial increase in enrolment in the period of 2001-2011. It is also found that the public schools are still more popular than private schools for the higher secondary education. It is also found that the private tuitions make countless students uninterested in taking admission in the private higher secondary schools. It was found that up to 1970 there were no private higher secondary school in the whole of South Kashmir region and the first private higher secondary school were established in the year 1971.

SECTION – B
CHANGING POLICIES OF THE STATE AND VARIOUS PRIVATE INSTITUTIONS OF EDUCATION

Modern system of education in India was started for the first time in 1835 when they first took up the responsibility of educating the citizens and financing of education in India. Before this we largely had informal modes of education and the concept of English education was alien to most parts of India. Since the education in India was largely unorganized and also the imparting of education took place in various different mediums of education a need for a uniform system which needs to be implemented all across the country was strongly felt by the then British Government. In order to realize this aim of standardization of education, commissions headed by eminent people from the sector have been appointed to formulate guidelines on how to standardize the education in the country. The first commission which has been established in this regard was the commission which was headed by Lord Macaulay in 1835. After this subsequently a number of commissions have been appointed by the government to give recommendations and guidelines for the improvement of education qualitatively and quantitatively in India. The British Indian Government took steps to implement the recommendations in the then British India and also princely states like Jammu and Kashmir which were ruled by their own rulers. After the attainment of independence the Indian Government also appointed the commissions on a regular basis to initiate reforms in the education sector. The government of Jammu and Kashmir has also appointed state specific commissions, programs and policies to bring about a change in the system of education in the state. The study of these commissions and their recommendations gives us a fair idea about the status of the education in the particular period of time and also show the problems plaguing the system and the steps taken to change them. Thus a brief study of all the commissions, programs and policies is imperative to understand the history of education in India and especially the state of Jammu and Kashmir. In order to access the objective number 2 of the present study, the data is divided in to two parts: Pre Independent Era and Post Independent Era.

POLICIES IN PRE INDEPENDENCE ERA

1. *Macaulay's Minutes (1835)*

Lord Macaulay came to India as a law member of the council of governor general on June 10, 1834. He was a learned scholar of English literature and a very fluent orator. He was appointed chairman of the society of public instructions of Bengal by Lord William Bentinck. Macaulay put on end to this controversy through his famous minutes in Feb. 1835 about medium of instruction. In this minute he supported western education through English medium in India.

Main Features of Macaulay's Minutes

Meaning of the word "literature": In the charter of 1813 the word 'Literature' meant English 'Literature' and not Sanskrit or Arabic or Persian literature.

Indian scholar: Indian scholar meant a scholar who is learnt in the Locke's philosophy, Milton's poetry, i.e., English literature. Hence, Indians should gain through knowledge of English Literature and Western philosophy.

Medium of instruction: Criticizing the native literature and languages, Lord Macaulay advocated English to be made. Therefore, Macaulay discarded the local languages and degraded these literatures. He cracked many malicious jokes on Sanskrit literature, which proved his ignorance of it.

Stoppage of grants to oriental schools: Macaulay said that if government felt that its old educational policy has failed, it can change its policy and stop the grants.

Religious concept: Macaulay was strictly secular minded. He did not like to interfere with the religions of Indians in any way.

Proposal for preparing code in English: Macaulay was not in favor of the study of Hindu and Islamic Law through Sanskrit, Arabic and Persian. He called it a foolishness to continue oriental institutions for the knowledge of laws. He proposed to get all the law books of Sanskrit and Arabic and Persian translated into English and prepare the code of laws.

Advocacy of downward filtration theory: Downward filtration theory regarding the education of masses was advocated. Here English would be of immense help to this.

2. *Wood's Dispatch (1854)*

Wood's educational dispatch, popularly known as Wood's dispatch is the corner stone of Indian education. It was so comprehensive that it contained a scheme of education for all Indians. It was for the first time in the annals of India that parliament investigated seriously into educational affairs of the country. Westernization had set in and along with it gave birth to nationalism which gradually swept the whole thought of one nationality despite diversities.

Main Recommendations

Acceptance of educational responsibility: Wood's Dispatch placed the responsibility of education of the Indian people fully on the company and stated quite explicitly that it must never be neglected.

Aim of education: Education is to raise intellectual fitness and moral character of Indians. At the same time it was to prepare them to become supporters of British rule in India.

Oriental languages: Mr. Wood had recognized the usefulness of 'Sanskrit', 'Arabic' and 'Persian' and recommended them as subjects of study in regular institutions. Like Macaulay, he also recognized the usefulness of western knowledge for Indians.

Medium of instruction: The Dispatch recommended that due to the shortage of books in Indian languages, the medium of instruction should be English. But English should be needed for those people who have proper knowledge and taste for English and are able to understand European knowledge through this language. For others Indian languages should be used.

Establishment of education department: The Dispatch directed that department of public instruction should be established in every province. Its highest authority would be the director of public instruction.

Establishment of universities: The Dispatch recommended the establishment of universities in presidency towns of Calcutta, Bombay and Madras, and if necessary at other places too.

Establishment of graded schools: The Dispatch recommended that there should be graded schools all over the country.

Grant-in-aid system: Charles Wood recommended that the system of grant-in-aid should be started with definite rules to encourage private enterprise to open educational institutions and proposed the sanction for grant-in-aid to the educational institutions of India for increase in teacher's salaries, scholarships, libraries and construction of building etc.

Education of women, Muslim education and Vocational education: Charles Wood threw light on women education, Muslim education and vocational education and suggested for its further encouragement through grant-in-aid and other measures.

3. *Hunter Commission (1882)*

On February 3, 1882, Lord Rippon came to India. He appointed the first Indian Education Commission, with Mr. Hunter, a member of the viceroy's executive council, as the chairman. Therefore, it came to be popularly known as 'Hunter Commission'.

Recommendation

Primary education and curriculum: Primary education should aim not only at preparing the students to enter into higher education but it should aim at spreading public education to all. Regarding primary education, Hunter Commission recommended that subjects such as physics, agriculture, first aid, banking, geometry etc. which have practical role in life should be included in the curriculum.

Financial administration: The commission suggested that local bodies should ear mark a certain amount for this job. It was also recommended that the provisional governments should give some aid for this.

Establishment of the training institutions: The commission recommended that in order to raise the standard of the primary institutions, the teachers should be properly trained. It recommended the opening of the normal schools.

Indigenous education: According to Hunter Commission only those institutions should be called indigenous institutions, 'patshalas" that are run by Indians according to the Indian tradition of education.

Secondary education: In the field of secondary education Hunter Commission tendered its opinion over the ways and means through which secondary education may be improved and also for improving on the defects in it.

Expansion: The commission recommended that in order to expend the secondary education, the government through the system of grant-in-aid should give the administration and organization of secondary education into the hands of efficient and able Indians, and get itself relieved of the responsibilities of running secondary education.

Curriculum: The Commission recommended that the curriculum of the secondary education should be split up into two parts, one that has subjects that are useful for higher study and the other which have vocational, occupational and practical subjects.

Medium of instruction: As regards the medium of instruction the commission said that English should continue as medium of instruction at the secondary stage of education.

Higher education: The commission also made recommendations in regard to higher education. These recommendations may be summed up as follows:

a. The number of teachers, expenditure of the college efficiency and local needs must also be kept in mind while giving grants-in-aid to the colleges.

b. Meritorious and promising students may be sent to foreign countries for higher education on government scholarship.

c. To raise the moral standards of the students, such books should be compiled which may contain the principles of human religion at large.

d. As compared to government colleges, private colleges should be authorized to receive lesser fee.

Education department: Hunter Commission had recommended that the number of inspectors in every province should be raised so that every institution may be inspected and that Indians should be appointed on the post of district inspectors of schools as for as possible, also they should be local people as far as possible.

System of grant-in-aid: Hunter Commission had made recommendations for the changes and reforms in the rule of grant-in-aid system, keeping in view the condition and requirements of all the institutions of the state.

Women education, Muslim education and education of backward classes: Arrangement for public fund, liberal grant-in-aid, public co-operation, free education, lady inspectors, special arrangements for education of 'parda' observing ladies and decent arrangements of hostels and different curriculum for girls.

4. *Indian Universities Commission (1902)*

There were two important reasons for the appointment of the commission. The defects of the university education were very glaring and nothing had been done to remodel The Indian Universities since they were established and the matter was left untouched by the Indian Education Commission of 1882.

Major Recommendations

i.   Instead of recognizing the universities, the senate and syndicate should be recognized. The members of the senate should be reduced and their terms should be five years and there should be a proper representation of the teachers and the scholars of the affiliated colleges in the university senate.

ii.   There should be proper arrangement for teaching in the college's affiliated to the universities, and the rules for recognition should be strictly observed and enforced and the affiliated colleges should be strictly supervised by the universities.

iii.   Universities should appoint teachers to impart higher education.

iv.   Hostels should be built for the students and according to the position of the students; the arrangement for scholarships should take place.

v.   The standard of the metric examination should be high so as to abolish the inter examination and also the curriculum of B.A should be of three years.

vi.   A managing committee should be there for every college which besides managing the college concerned, should also appoint competent teachers and pay attention towards the discipline of the students and the construction of buildings and hostels etc.

5. *Indian Universities Act (1904)*

Lord Curzon accorded the top priority in his program of educational reforms to university education reform. For this task he appointed the Indian Universities Commission (1902) to enquire into the conditions of universities, to consider and report upon proposals for improving their constitution and working. After the submission of the report, the Indian Universities Act was passed on March 21, 1904 in The Imperial Legislative Council in the face of bitter opposition. The act, by and large, embodied the main recommendations of the commission. It also included the main suggestions of the government of India's Resolution on Indian educational policy.

Main Provisions

i.   Universities were given the right of teaching along with the right of conducting examinations also and the right to appoint teachers.

ii. Prior to this, the number of seats in the senate of the universities not fixed and the government used to make life-long nominations. According to this act, the minimum number was fifty and the maximum number was hundred and their term was determined for five years.

iii. The members of the senate got the right to elect members. Such elected members, were not to be more than 20 for The Universities of Calcutta, Bombay and Madras and 15 for other universities.

iv. Legal status was given to the syndicates of the universities and in these syndicates proper representation of professors was made compulsory. The government secured the right to make amendments and reforms and give approval to the rules framed by the senates of the universities.

v.   In order to raise the standards of education, the syndicate could cause the inspection of the colleges imparting higher education.

6. *Education in Jammu and Kashmir Issues and Documents (Report of the Sharp Committee 1916)*

In 1916 Maharaja Pratap Singh invited Sir Henry Sharp, the Educational Commissioner, Government of India, to suggest various ways and means to extend educational facilities for the Muslims of Kashmir.

Major Recommendations

i. According to the report, the further expansion of primary education was "a prime necessity". In view of the paucity of Muslim pupils, the committee recommended some scholarship for Muslim students.

ii. Mr. Sharp remarked that the problem of practical education was one of the most urgent and important issues with which the Maharaja had to deal.

iii. The establishment of a few college scholarships of Rs. 10 for Muslims was also suggested. Such a proposal was supposed to have a good effect on the Muslim community.

iv. Mr. Sharp suggested that it would do well if a Muslim teacher of good qualifications could be added to the Shri Partap College in Srinagar as opportunity offered and, as soon as possible, to the state high school in the city.

v. "Owing to the poverty of the Muslim community," remarked Mr. Sharp".

vi. 'some special concession by way of grant was justifiable in the case of Islamic schools, whether primary, middle or high.'

vii. Grant paid to private institutions may be enhanced. The grants should be raised to Rupees 10 thousand a year.

viii. The State may open a training class for (audio-visual) teachers who are deputed outside at one of its colleges.

7. *Calcutta University Commission (Sadlar Commission) 1917*

In 1917 The Government of India appointed The Calcutta University Commission, which was asked "to enquire into the conditions and prospects of the University of Calcutta and to consider the question of a constructive policy in relation to it. Sir Michal Sadlar, the vice-chancellor of Leads University was appointed as its chairman thus popularly known as Sadlar Commission. The members of the committee were Indian Educationists as well as British such as Asutosh Mookerji, Ramsay Murty, Philp Hartong etc.

Recommendations

i. The commission recommended that there should be an intermediary link between secondary and higher education and therefore, intermediate colleges be created imparting instruction in arts, science, agriculture and commerce etc. Mother tongue should be the medium of instruction at intermediate stage.

ii. For proper management and control of school education, the commission recommended for the establishment of a Board of High school and intermediate education in each province.

iii. A three year degree course should be instituted and intermediate classes should be separated from the university.

iv. Government control over The Universities should be less and flexible and an academic council should be set up.

v. University teachers should be appointed by Selection Committee constituted especially for the purpose.

vi. Degree course was to be of three years and Provisions should be made for imparting instructions in Engineering Education, Medicine, Law, Agriculture etc.

vii. The number of Trained Teachers should be increased without any delay and Departments of Education should be created at the Universities of Calcutta and Dacca.

viii. The government should start 'Parda' schools for those girls whose parents have a desire to educate their daughters upto the age of 15 or 16

ix. Co-education should be encouraged at such places where there were no separate institutions of the girls.

x. Special provisions for the training of women teachers should be made and provisions should be made for medical courses for women.

xi. The commission felt that education should not only prepare the boys for government posts, it should also encourage them to have technological and Vocational Education.

8. *Forming of the Glancy Commission 1932*

During late 20's and early thirties of this century there were complaints that the things in various walks of State- life were not going on properly. As a result Maharaja Han Singh appointed a commission to study the cause of the grievances of people and to make recommendations. Though the commission was not directly related to education, it made important recommendations regarding this area as well.

Major Recommendations

i.   The expansion of primary education should be accelerated and more attention should be paid to the provision of suitable buildings for primary schools;

ii.   The request of the Muslims of Jammu to have an. Islamic High School in Gandoo Di Chawani deserves, favorable consideration

iii. A regular programme for the construction of middle schools and high schools should be drawn up;

iv.   That a higher proportion of the special Mohammedan scholarships grant should be allotted to high schools and colleges rather than to middle schools, in order to encourage higher education among Muslims;

v.   Efforts should be made to increase the number of Muslim employees in the teaching department. A special Muhammadan inspector should be appointed: to attend to the progress of Muhammadan education in all grades.

9. *Punjab University Enquiry Committee Report 1933*

In October 1932, the Government of Punjab appointed an enquiry committee to study the situation in Punjab University regarding its functioning since Jammu and Kashmir State was also under the territorial jurisdictions of Punjab University. The recommendations made by the committee, particularly regarding courses of study are relevant to J&K state as well:

Major Recommendations

i. In primary stage efforts have to be made to render the system more efficient and to reduce alarming wastage which obtains in all provinces.

ii. The secondary course in vernacular schools should be increased by one year.

iii. The present intermediate classes of the colleges and class X of the schools should be included in separate self contained higher secondary institutions, the courses for which would thus extend over three years.

iv. Students' fees should be uniform and proportionate to the cost of institute. . A maximum age limit for entrance should be imposed.

v. A board of higher secondary education should be constituted by legislation. A university board of affiliated colleges should be constituted.

10. *Wardha or Basic Scheme of Education "Nai Talim (Gandhiji) 1937*

Basic scheme of Education which was conceived and explained by Mahatma Gandhi is essentially education for life and education through life. It is also called as "Nai Talim" "Wardha Scheme". Basic stands for fundamentals. It means that this scheme of education was based on the national culture and civilization of India. It shall have close relationship with the basic needs and interest of the child life and is associated with the main occupation of the community life of the country. The central pivot of the scheme of education shall be some handicrafts whose teaching shall enable the students to be able to solve the problems of his livelihood.

Fundamentals of basic scheme of education: Basic scheme of education is a dynamic and progressive scheme and is based on the psychological and sociological factors. The various fundamentals of the scheme are discussed as follows:-

Free and compulsory education for children from seven to 14 years: Education should be free and compulsory from the age of seven to fourteen years.

Mother tongue to be the medium of instruction: He stressed that mother tongue should be the medium of instruction. He believed that no real education is possible through a foreign medium.

Craft as the centre of education: Education should centre round some productive craft. It must have educative possibilities and provide the nucleus of all other instruction provided in the school.

Self supporting element: The scheme of Basic education is based on the principle "Learn while you earn and earn while you learn".

Cult of non-violence: Gandhi ji emphasized the principle of non-violence in every field of life.

The ideal of a co-operative community: The scheme envisages the idea of a cooperative community, in which the motive of social service will dominate all the activities of children during the plastic years of child-hood and youth.

Relationship with life: Education should be closely related to life. Everything is to be taught the principle of correlation.

11. *Education Reorganization Committee 1938-39 (Saiyidain Committee Report)*

During the early thirties of this century there was a popular upsurge for education in Jammu And Kashmir State. By this time the scheme of Basic Education was formulated and was gaining popularity. The state government was desirous to adopt the scheme. Dr. Zakir Hussain was invited in this state to head of the Department of Education; since he was not free to accept the offer Mr. K.G Saiyidain was appointed. An education reconstruction committee was founded.

Major Recommendations

i.   The new scheme of education propounded by the Committee aimed at the establishment of a system of free compulsory and universal basic education for all the children in the State not below the age of 7.

ii. According to the report, the most important problem in educational reorganization was the improvement in the quality and the efficiency of the teaching personnel. Such a policy was bound to encourage the growth and development of private institutions.

iii. The committee advocated a diversification of the secondary course and the introduction of more practical work. A scheme of education should be drawn up in which craft teaching and book teaching should be given simultaneously.

iv. Provision should be made for construction of 100 buildings every year for basic primary schools, for, crafts needed specially constructed houses.

v. Adequate arrangements should be made for the proper training of teachers. Facilities for adult education should be augmented. Village libraries should be raised from 50 to 100 and adult education centers raised from50 to 100 in each province.

vi. With regard to girl's education, the committee recommended that 20 primary and 4 middle schools should be opened every year instead of 2 middle schools and 6 primary schools.

12. *Sargent Report (1944)*

Sargent Scheme of Education has a historical importance from the point of view of development of "National Education System". This was the first report that presented a comprehensive picture of education in India.

Recommendations regarding pre-primary education: Nursery schools should be started for the success of National Scheme of Education. These nurseries may be attached to Junior Basic Schools in rural areas. In the urban areas where there is sufficient number of children these nursery schools should have separate existence. Pre-primary education should be free.

Recommendations regarding primary education: The committee recommended free and compulsory Primary or Basic education to the children of the age group of 6-14. This education should be based on some craft. Basic schools were divided into two categories: Junior Basic Schools and Senior Basic Schools and the mother tongue should be the medium of instruction of Junior and senior basic schools. In the Junior Basic Schools, there should be one teacher for every 30 students while as it should be 25 at senior level.

Recommendations regarding secondary education: Their abilities, interests, aptitudes etc should be borne in mind while giving them admission. 50% students shall be given free education. It has also been recommended to given scholarships to the poor students, so that they may not be deprived of this stage of education. Mother tongue should be the medium of instruction and English should be taught as a second compulsory subject. This scheme of education has recommended that the aim of Secondary education should be to make the boys self dependent and be able to stand on their own legs.

Recommendations regarding higher education: Sargent scheme of education suggested a three year degree course. In order to raise the standard of university education, the scheme has recommended the appointment of competent teachers, improvement in salary scales and reforms in the conditions of service. There should be close contact between the teacher and the student. There should be strict rules for admission to universities. The scheme has suggested for the appointments of University Grants Commission and introduction of tutorial system.

Recommendations regarding technical industrial and vocational education: A great stress has been laid on industrial and vocational education under this scheme. Provisions are to be made for the higher category of workers and lower category of workers and training should be given to them. Skilled and semi skilled craftsmen are very much needed for successful execution of industrial and occupational schemes.

Recommendations regarding adult education: Sargent Report made recommendations in regard to the education of uneducated adults from 10-40 years. It is said that adult Education is very much essential for the success of the ideal of democratic way of life.

Recommendations regarding training of teachers: It was suggested to conduct refresher course for all the categories of the teachers. It was suggested to improve the salary scales of the teachers and provide them free training to them in the training colleges and schools.

Recommendations regarding the education of handicapped: It was suggested to start special institutions for the education of the students physically or psychologically handicapped.

Suggestions regarding the health education of students: The report attached great importance to the health of the children. It was suggested to provide physical education and due medical checkup and treatment to the students of 6 to 14 years of age.

POLICIES IN POST INDEPENDENCE ERA

1. *Radha Krishnan Commission, 1948*

On August 15, 1947 India became free from the foreign yoke. A national government was formed at the centre and the work on framing a new constitution started. For the development of Education, the government of India appointed various committees and commissions with the sole purpose of bringing about drastic changes in the education system of the country. A commission under the chairmanship of the ex-president of India, Dr. Radha Krishnan was appointed in 1948 with the sole objective of suggesting suitable reforms in the field of higher education. Eminent educationists like Dr. Zakir Hussain, Dr. Siddhant, Dr. Tara Chand and other veterans were members of the commission. A brief description of main recommendations is given below:

Recommendations

i. The commission dealt at length with regard to the qualifications, pay scales, conditions of work and service conditions, training and other problems connected with the teachers of the universities and affiliated colleges.

ii. It prescribed healthy suggestions for raising the quality and standard of teaching and research in higher education and the commission recommended the division of the curriculum into general, literacy and vocational categories keeping in view the interests, aptitude and inclination of students.

iii. The commission gave important recommendations for the development of professional, technical and industrial education. It recommended for the adoption of three-language formula as the medium of instruction.

iv. Due place was given to religious and moral education in the curriculum aimed at creating a feeling of unity and amity among all religions and through it to foster a feeling of oneness.

v. The commission gave some useful suggestions with regard to the system of examination and evaluation with due emphasis on internal assessment.

vi. It suggested for the formation of student's bodies in the universities and colleges to look after the welfare of the students.

vii. For promoting agricultural education the commission recommended for the creation of agricultural universities and rural institutes on the pattern of Sweden and Denmark. It also presented a detailed plan for the development and expansion of women education in the country.

The University Grants Commission was created by government of India for providing liberal grants to universities and affiliated colleges for development and improvement.

2. *The Jammu & Kashmir University Act (1948)*

Whereas in view of the changed circumstance it is expedient to withdraw affiliation of the colleges and educational institutions of the state from the universities of Punjab and to establish at Srinagar, a teaching and examining university in the state and to provide for the affiliation of such colleges and institutions with the university.

Powers of the university

i. To hold examinations, to grant degrees and to confer other academic distinctions and to confer honorary degrees

ii. To grant such diplomas to, and to provide such lectures and instruction for persons not being members of the university as the university may determine.

iii. To admit and maintain colleges, to recognize colleges and other institutions, not maintained by the university and to withdraw such recognition

iv. To inspect affiliated colleges and other institutions and places approved by the University for Residence of students.

v. To supervise and control the residence and discipline of the students of the university of colleges or other institutions admitted or affiliated to it.

vi. To institute and award fellowships, exhibitions, prizes and medals.

vii. To do all such other things and acts as may be requisite in order to further the objects of the university as a teaching, affiliating and examining body.

3. *Committee on the ways and Means of Financing Educational Development (1950)*

The 14th meeting of Central Advisory Board of Education and the All India Educational Conference held in January 1948 raised the question of future education program. It was generally agreed that the period of 40 years laid down in the report of "Post War Education Development" in India published in January 1944 must be curtailed and if necessary for the purpose, stage up to which compulsion should be enforced may also be reduced. It was, therefore, decided to appoint a Committee under the Chairmanship of Shri B.G Kher to examine and the program for educational development for all provinces and states and to make suggestions to ensure that educational development may not be held up for want of funds.

Recommendations

i.   The state must undertake the responsibility of providing at least junior basic education for everybody.

ii.   The provinces should aim at introducing Universal Compulsory Education for the children of 6-11 age groups within a period of ten years.

iii. The basic minimum salary of trained basic school teachers should be rupees 40 per month and should on no account be reduced.

iv.   In urban areas, where conditions justify, the same school buildings should be used for two shifts provided different teachers are employed in each shift.

v.   Voluntary efforts should be encouraged for meeting the capital and recurring cost of education and voluntary organizations should be induced to run educational institutions with such assistance from Government as may be feasible.

vi.   Wherever conditions permit, loan should be raised for meeting the capital cost of such part there of as may be necessary and about 70% of the expenditure on education should be borne by the local bodies and provinces and the remaining 30% by the centre.

vii. All contributors for education approved by the provincial or Central Government should be exempted from income-tax.

4. *Mudaliar Commission, 1952*

The commission was named after its chairman, Dr. A. Lakshaman Swami Mudaliar. He was the permanent vice-chancellor of Madras University and an eminent educationist. The commission is popularly known as Secondary Education commission because it aimed at bringing about important reforms in the field of secondary education in the country.

Recommendations

i.   The commission recommended for the re-organization of the system of education at primary-Junior and secondary level. It recommended 4 or 5 years primary, 3 years senior basic and 3 years secondary education in the country. It laid special emphasis on diversification of courses at the secondary level.

ii. It emphasized on opening schools for the handicapped and backward children including deaf, dumb, blind and retarded ones.

iii. The commission recommended that at the secondary stage each student should study at least two languages among them one should be mother tongue or regional language and the scope of secondary curriculum needed to be widened.

iv. For raising the quality of text-books, high power committees should be constituted both in the centre and states and dynamic methods of teaching and audiovisual aids should be used.

v.   Facilities of proper guidance and counseling should exist in educational institutions.

vi. In examinations, the new concepts of evaluation should be adopted.

5. *Committee on Differentiation of Curricula for Boys and Girls (1961-1964)*

The National Council for Women's education, in its meeting held on May 10, 1961 authorized its chairman to set up a committee to examine comprehensively the problem of curricula for girls at all stages of Education. The Chairman Smt. Raksha Saran, set up the committee on Nov 1, 1961 in consultation with the Ministry of Education. The committee consisted of 11 members. Smt. Hansa Mehta was the chairperson of the committee.

Recommendations

Sex difference: According to the traditional view the mere biological difference of sex created different physical, intellectual and psychological characteristics between men and women and these basic sex differences necessitated the provision of differentiated curricula for them.

Equality of women: The existing gap between the education of boys and girls should be rapidly bridged. Intensive efforts should be made to educate the public regarding the scientific findings about sex differences and to develop proper attitudes in each sex towards the order.

Co-education: Co-education should be adopted as the general pattern at the elementary stage. At the secondary and collegiate stages, there should be full freedom to the managements and parents either to evolve common institutions or to establish separate ones for girls.

Proposals for differentiation of curricula

Primary stage: No differentiation should be made in the curricula for boys and girls at the Primary Stage. Women should be appointed on the staff of all primary schools.

Middle school stage: The curriculum of general education should be common to boys and girls and no differentiation should be made therein on the basis of sex. In all middle schools it is desirable to have mixed staff

Secondary stage: Sex education is essential at the middle and secondary stage. There should be introduction of home science in the secondary school curriculum.

Vocational education: Immediate attempts should be directed to expand the provision of vocational courses at the secondary and higher stages of education.

6. *Indian Education Commission (Kothari Commission) 1964-66*

To throw light on the comprehensive and integrated aspect of education and to suggest measures for its development and improvement, the Government of India appointed a Commission in 1964 under the chairmanship of Dr. D.S Kothari, the then Chairman of University Grants Commission (UGC), Delhi. The commission consisted of several eminent Indian educationists. After visiting different parts of the country and collected relevant data, the commission submitted its report in 1966. It provided a detailed plan of two decades (1966-1986) for the development of Education for the country. The name of the report is popularly known as "Education and National Development". It provided the development of education according to national development.

Recommendations

Education and national objectives: The commission felt that the most important and urgent reform needed in education is to transform it, an endeavor to relate it to the life, needs and aspirations of the people and thereby make it a powerful instrument of social, economic and cultural transformation necessary for the realization of the national goals. For this purpose the commission recommended that education should be developed so as to increase productivity and achieve social and national integration, accelerate the process of modernization and cultivate social, moral and spiritual values.

Education and productivity: The commission gave following programs to relate education to productivity: Science education, work experience and vocational education.

Social and national integration: The following steps should be taken to strengthen national consciousness and unity: common school system, social and national service, medium of instruction.

Education and modernization: To modernize itself, a society has to educate itself. Apart from raising the education level of the average citizens, it must try to create an intelligentsia of adequate size and competence which comes from all strata of society and whose loyalties and aspirations are rooted to the Indian soil.

Social, moral and spiritual values: The commission recommended that education should be emphasized for the development of fundamental, social, moral and spiritual values. The central and state governments should adopt measures for that in all institutions.

Teacher education: Education should be organized as an independent academic discipline and introduced as an elective subject in courses for the first and second degree. Summer institutes should be organized for the in-service training of staff.

Teacher's status: Kothari Commission 1966 gave healthy suggestions for the improvement of teaching and education. For the social, economic and professional growth of teachers the commission suggested radical reforms with regard to their qualifications, pay scale and conditions of work and service.

School curriculum: With regard to curriculum, the commission recommended mother-tongue, math's, science, health education, social studies and creative activities as the teaching subjects for children at primary stage. At the higher primary apart from other subjects, two languages, art, in calculation of the spiritual values, work experience and social service should be included in the curriculum.

Higher education: In the field of higher education, at the outset, the commission made a special reference to the objectives of setting up universities. According to the commission, the chief aim of a university should be to search and develop new knowledge. All should work freely and fearlessly for the research for finding out the truth and attainment of excellence and also give a thrust for agricultural, technical, adult and vocational education.

7. *Report of the Education Reorganization Committee 1967 (Kazemi Committee Report)*

After achieving independence the Prime Minister (now called Chief Minister) took over the portfolio of education as a practical symbol of importance he attached to education in the building up of new order of things in Kashmir. He therefore appointed a committee which could reorganize the system of education in order to meet the needs and aspirations of "New Kashmir". The work of Educational Reorganization Committee began on 18th of August, 1950 when the Prime Minister addressed the committee on the new problems of education in Jammu and Kashmir State. The committee submitted its report on 4th December, 1950.

Recommendations

The committee approved to give due importance to kindergarten teaching. The science and art of the development of very young children through kindergarten is now so universally recognized that it is no longer a fad for rich man's children. It must, however, be adapted to the needs of the poorest. A concerted drive to make the primary stage effective would involve retraining of teachers. Craft and handwork should form an integral part of the primary syllabus.

Secondary schools: Adequate thought went into secondary school education. All agreed that the present aimless drift of boys with the educational stream must stop. Whatever a boy's particular aptitude, he tended to attempt to pass matriculation and enter college with some vague idea of getting state service at the end of his labors. This resulted in mental frustration for the boys and in a good deal of available unemployment.

Curricula: Mother tongue as medium at the primary stage. Regional language as medium at the secondary stage, English medium at the university stage with the federal language as one of the compulsory subject.

Changes in the girl's curriculum: The committee felt that an important and necessary change in the curriculum should be to make home science a compulsory subject for all girls up to the matriculation standard.

Taking training to the teachers: Training should be taken to the teachers rather than expecting all of them to come to the training institutions where only limited seats is available.

Salaries and promotions: The Prime Minister said that if the teacher was expected to give his best to the teaching of the younger generation he must be better paid.

Co-operation and education: It is understood that the rapidly developing co-operative movement has a fund for educational purposes and this fund should be used both in villages and towns for the equipment and building of schools in the localities from which money had been collected.

Physical education: Everyone recognizes the necessity of having good arrangements for physical education, but unfortunately, both in school and colleges there is very little qualified and capable staff which can deal with this side of educational activity. Girls' schools are particularly lake in facilities. Even where certain exercises are gone through, they are selected to give a superficial atmosphere of smartness and they make no contribution to the scientific building of a healthy body.

8. *The Private Educational Institutions (Regulations & Control) Act 1967*

Appointment of Competent Authority: The Government may by notification in the Government Gazette, appoint one or more persons having prescribed qualifications to be the competent authority or authorities for the purposes of this Act and define the area within which each such authority shall exercise its jurisdiction.

Permission of competent authority: No institutions shall be established or run except with the permission in writing of the competent authority.

Application for permission: The sponsor of every institution existing at the commencement of this Act shall make an application to the competent authority for permission to run such institution as the case may be. .

Grant of permission: On receipt of application, the competent authority may grant or refuse to grant permission to the sponsor of the institution applying for such permission after taking into account the following matters:

(a) The method of imparting   instructions.

(b) The qualifications of the members of teaching staff.

(c) Provisions for library and laboratory

(d) The suitability and adequacy of accommodations.

(e) The provisions for the welfare of the students

List of private educational institutions to be published: The Government shall on or before the first May of each year, publish in the Government Gazette a list containing the names of every institution which has been granted permission   The Government shall publish in the Government Gazette as soon as possible the name of such institutions in respect of which such permission has been cancelled under this Act.

Accounts: Every approved institution (recognized under this Act) shall keep accounts in such a manner and containing such particulars as may be prescribed.

Audit: The accounts of every approved institution having an annual income of not less than Rs 6,000 shall be audited annually by an auditor to be appointed by the Government.

Directions: The competent authority may from time to time issue such directions regarding the management of approved institutions as it may think fit and it shall be the duty of the sponsor of such institution to carry out such directions within such time as may be fixed on this behalf by the competent authority.

Appeal: Any sponsor aggrieved by the decision of the competent authority may prefer an appeal to the Government against such decision within a period of 30 days from the date such decision is conveyed to him.

Penalties: Whosoever contravenes any of the provisions of this Act shall be punishable with fine which may extend to five thousand rupees.

Power to make rules: The Government may by notification in the Government Gazette make rules to carry out the purposes of this Act.

9. *Bhagwan Sahayi Committee-1972 (J&K)*

After independence a number of commissions were appointed to re-organize different stages of education in India. In Jammu & Kashmir also need was felt to bring about these changes. Consequently, the Government of Jammu & Kashmir appointed an Education Committee under the chairman ship of Shri Bhagwan Sahay, the Governor of Jammu & Kashmir for the re-organization of education system in the state. It is after his name, the committee is known as Bhagwan Sahay Committee (1972).

Recommendations of the committee:

i.   The committee recommended that secondary education should be strengthened through careful planning of location of secondary schools lengthening its duration to four years, transfer of pre university course and the first year of third degree course to secondary schools and the development of a large scale program of diversification and vocational education.

ii.   The committee also recommended that new and dynamic method of teaching should be adopted.

iii. Special emphasis should be laid on the education of girls and women. The trend towards adoption of co-education should be encouraged.

iv.   The committee recommended that there should be an autonomous organization for the production, distribution and sale of text books.

v. The Bhagwan Sahai committee recommended that good training colleges be established in all districts for primary and middle school teachers.

vi. The committee recommended that an officer of adequate status should be appointed in the department of education to look after the programs of teacher's education. It also recommends that a State Board of Teacher Education should be established.

vii. The committee recommended that curriculum should be revised and upgraded at the school stage with special emphasis on work experience.

viii. The committee recommended that three year honors' courses should be started at the under graduate stage.

ix. The committee recommended that residential accommodation should be provided for teachers, wherever necessary.

x. The Bhagwan Sahai Committee recommended that academic calendar in the state should be re-organized

xi. Private educational institutions should be regulated on the board lines recommended by the Education Commission.

10. *The Jammu and Kashmir Board of School Education Act, 1975*

The Board shall be a body corporate by the name of the "Jammu and Kashmir State Board of School Education" shall have perpetual succession and a common seal and shall have power to acquire, hold and dispose of property and to enter into contracts and do all other things necessary for the purpose of its constitution and may sue or be sued by its corporate name as aforesaid.

Powers and functions of the board

i. To prescribe the courses of institution, prepare curricula and detailed syllabi and also prescribe text books for the elementary, secondary school and higher secondary (school graduation), school examinations,

ii. To conduct public examinations for persons who have pursued the secondary school and higher secondary (school graduation) school education courses and to publish the results of examinations conducted by the Board,

71

iii. To recognize institutions for the purpose of providing instructions in the secondary and higher secondary burses on such conditions and on receipt of such fees as may be fixed by the regulations,

iv. To conduct inspection of the recognized schools/institutions to ensure that the recognized schools have the requisite facilities of playground, furniture, laboratories, library, equipment, accommodation and qualified teaching staff as prescribed by the regulations,

v. To hold control and administer the funds and property by the Board and to receive bequests, donations, endowments, trusts and other transfers of any property or, interest therein,

vi. To co-operate with the University of Jammu, University of Kashmir, and other Boards and with other authorities and with other institutions in such manner and for such purposes as the Board may determine,

vii. To call for reports from a Director of School Education on the conditions prevailing in the recognized institutions or in institutions applying for recognition and to adopt means to promote the physical, moral, cultural and social welfare of the students in recognized institutions,

viii. To exercise full academic control over, the recognized institutions.

11. *Report of the Kashmir University Committee (Tayabji Committee Report 1978)*

The University Grants Commission at the suggestion of the State, Government of Jammu & Kashmir appointed committee to review the working of the University of Kashmir.

Recommendations

i. An inter-university coordination and policy council should be set up by the state government as a statutory body. The functions of the executive council and the Syndicate should be combined.

ii. There should be a senate to serve as a forum for various sections of the community to meet and discuss the broad policies and programs of the university.

iii. The academic council should primarily deal with policy matters relating to academic development. There should be separate boards of studies for undergraduates and post-graduate studies including research

iv. The act may authorize the transfer of administrative staff including the registrar and controller of examinations between the two state Universities, or to comparable positions in university centre, colleges or the state education department.

v. The benefits of higher education may be spread in rural areas by organizing extension and adult education programs, and providing technical know-how, wherever possible, for developing rural crafts and trades.

vi. For the development of higher studies in outlying and under-developed areas of the state, worth-while scholarships should be offered. Honors' courses should be started in a few selected colleges in the state.

vii. The university's admission procedure should be streamlined. Free hostel facilities need not be provided for all students. A women's hostel should be set up on the campus.

viii. The maintenance grant of State universities should be determined by the state government well in advance.

ix. The salary scales of the university and college teachers including the registrar, the deputy registrar, etc. should be on par with the scales recommended by the University Grants Commission and accepted by the central government.

x. University departments designated as centers may be grouped into schools and inter-disciplinary research programs encouraged.

xi. A law college should be established at Srinagar by the state government for providing degree level instruction in law.

xii. The study of linguistics should be introduced as a part of the language courses and also a course in Indian humanities should be introduced

xiii. The university library should build up a complete collection of documents and published material on all aspects of the Jammu and Kashmir state as possible and a publication unit should be set up.

xiv. To improve the educational standards and facilities of the colleges, the university should setup a college development council. And also should undertake specific programs including refresher courses.

12. *The Jammu & Kashmir Private Colleges (Regulation & Control) Act, 1984*

An act to provide for the regulation and control of private colleges in the state was enacted by the Jammu and Kashmir state legislature in the thirty-fifth year of the Republic of India.

i. No private college shall be established, run or maintained without the prior permission, in writing, of the government,

ii. The government shall prescribe the procedure to be followed for the grant of permission to establish, run or maintain private college

iii. Existing colleges shall be deemed to be recognized for a period of one year from the date of commencement of this act, there after they shall have to follow the prescribed procedure.

iv. The government may, at its discretion give grant-in-aid to the recognized private colleges. The quantum of such grant-in-aid and the conditions to be fulfilled by the private colleges for the receipt of such grant-in aid shall be prescribed by the government

v. All private colleges recognized under this act and duly registered with the government shall be maintained and run by the educational agencies in the prescribed manner.

vi. All selections and appointments of teaching staff in aided colleges shall be made by an appointment committee which shall be constituted by the government

vii. The conditions of service of teaching and non-teaching staff in aided colleges including conditions relating to pay, gratuity, provident fund and age or retirement shall be such as may be prescribed by the government.

viii. Where any college has been taken over under sub- section (2) the educational agency may subsequently apply to the government for the restoration of the college. The college may be restored when the government is satisfied that the educational agency is in a position to run the college satisfactorily.

ix. The government shall prescribe the manner in which the accounts of aided colleges shall be maintained

x.   The accounts of aided colleges shall be audited annually by an agency to be appointed by the government.

xi. The agency so appointed shall prepare report of the accounts and submit the same to the competent authority.

xii. The government may make rules for the purpose of carrying into effect the provisions of the act.

13. *The Jammu and Kashmir Education Act, 1984*

Whereas, it is expedient to achieve the goal of Universalization of elementary education and to provide better organization and development of school education in the state. Be it enacted by the Jammu and Kashmir state legislature in the third-fifth year plan of the Republic of India as follows:

i.   The provisions of this act shall apply to all schools in the state.

ii.   Compulsory education up to class eighth.

iii. The government may, for the purpose of providing adequate facilities for school education establish and maintain schools and permit any educational agency to establish and maintain private schools.

iv.   Government to prescribe manner in which government schools to be established and run

v.   The government may prescribe the grounds on which a child may be exempted from attending school.

vi.   No private school to be established or run without permission.

vii. The government shall prescribe the procedure to be followed for the grant of permission to establish, run or maintain private schools.

viii. The government shall prescribe norms and the minimum necessary conditions for the functioning of recognized schools.

ix.   The educational agency shall appoint a manager to look after the day to day running and administration of the school subject to the approval of the competent authority.

x.   All private schools shall have to seek the prior permission of the competent authority before adding any higher classes.

xi.   Property to be in the name of the educational agency.

xii.   All selections and appointments of teaching staff in aided schools shall be made by an appointments committee which shall be constituted by the government.

xiii.   The government may at its discretion give grant-in-aid to private schools. The manner in which the grant-in-aid is to be given and the conditions to be fulfilled by the schools for the receipt of such grant-in-aid shall be prescribed by the government.

xiv.   The government may make rules for the purpose of carrying into effect the provisions of the act.

14. *National Policy on Education, 1986 (New Education Policy)*

The National Policy on Education (1986) popularly known as the New Education Policy as a Magna Carta of the education for the days to come. The call for New Education Policy was first given by the Prime Minister of India Mr. Rajiv Gandhi in his broadcast to the nation of January 5, 1985. The final draft of the National Policy on Education was preceded by the 119 paged documents entitled 'Challenge of Education- A policy perspective' released by the Ministry of Education in August 1985. National Policy on Education was passed by the Lok Sabha on May 8 and Rajya Sabha on May 13, 1986. In August 1986, the Parliament approved the program of Action (1986) for giving shape to the new thrusts.

Main features of National Policy on Education (1986) Introductory

Education has continued to evolve, diversify and extend its reach and coverage since the dawn of human history. The country has reached the stage in its economic and technical development when a major effort must be made to derive the maximum benefits from the assets already created and to ensure that the fruits of change reach all sections. Education is the highway to that goal.

The essence and role of education: In our national perception, education is essential for all. This is fundamental to our all round development, material and spiritual. Education develops manpower for different levels of the country. Education is a unique investment in the present and the future.

National system of education: The concept of national system of education implies that up to a given level, all students, irrespective of caste, creed, location or sex have access to education of a comparable quality. National Circular Frame work which contains a common core along with other components in envisaged.

a. The 10+2+3 structure has now been accepted in all parts of the country.

b. In the higher education in general, and technical education in particular, inter- regional mobility. Education has to strengthen the world view and motivate the younger generation for international cooperation and peaceful co-existence.

c. Life -Long education is recognized and the role of National Institutions like UGC, AICTE, ICAR, IMC, NCERT, NIEPA is determined.

Education for equality: The new policy will lay special emphasis on the removal of disparities and to equalize educational opportunity be attending to the specific needs of those who have been denied equality so far.

Reorganization of education at different stages: The National Policy has included the following stages:

Early childhood care and education (ECCE): The National Policy on children specifically emphasis investment in the development of the young child, particularly children from sections of population in which first generation learners predominate.

Elementary education: Universal enrolment and universal reiteration of children up to 14 years age and a substantial improvement in the quality of education.

Secondary education: Secondary education begins to expose students to the differentiate roles of science, humanities and social science.

Higher education: Higher education provides people with an opportunity to reflect on the critical social, economic, cultural, moral and spiritual issues facing humanity. It contributes to national development through dissemination of specialized knowledge and skills.

Open University distance learning: The Open University system has been initiated in order to augment opportunities for higher education and as an instrument of democratizing education.

De-linking degrees for jobs: A beginning will be made in de-linking degrees from jobs in selected areas.

Rural University: The new pattern of the Rural University will be consolidated and developed on the lines of Mahatma Gandhi's revolutionary ideas on education so as to take up the challenges of micro-planning at grass root levels for the transformation of rural areas. Institutions and programs of Gandhi's basic education will be supported.

Technical and management education: Although the two streams of technical and management education are functioning separately, it is essential to look at them together in view of their close relationship and complementary concerns.

The teacher: The status of the teacher reflects the socio-cultural ethos of a society. It is said that no people can rise above the level of its teachers. Teachers should have the freedom to innovate, to devise appropriate methods of communication and activities relevant to the needs and capabilities of and the concerns of the community.

15. *Ramamurti Review Committee (1990)*

The short-lived Janata Government headed by Shri V.P.Singh, Prime Minister of India, appointed a committee on May 7, 1990 to review the National Policy on Education 1986, formulated by the Congress Government under Shri Rajiv Gandhi. The committee for review is popularly known as Ramamurti Review Committee after the name of Acharya Ramamurti who was the chairman of the committee. The committee submitted its report to the Minister of State in the Ministry of Human Resource Development on December 26, 1990 and the same was tabled to the parliament on January 9, 1991.

Recommendations

Development of common school system: A very vital component of the overall strategy for securing equity and social justice in education is the development of the common school system. Concrete steps for translating this concept into action have to be taken.

Removing disparities in education: The need of the hour is planning for, and implementation of education development programs in terms of disaggregated targets and area, community and gender specific activities. This would mean concrete programs being established on ground for the disadvantaged groups SC'S and ST'S, women, backward and handicapped.

Promotion of Women education: In order to promote participation of the girls and women in education at all levels, there is need for an integrated approach in designing and implementing the schemes that would address all the factors that inhabit their education.

Value education: In the view of the committee value education is to be constructed as a continuous process which is to be sustained throughout the process of growth of the individual from childhood to adolescence, then to adulthood and so on.

Early childhood care and education (ECCE): Free and compulsory education for all children until they complete the age of 14 years, should be enlarged to include early childhood care and education.

Right to education: The right to education should be examined for inclusion amongst the fundamental rights guaranteed under The Constitution of India. All the socio economic measures without which realization of this right will not be possible should be taken.

Work experience/socially useful productive work: Work experience/Socially useful productive work should be integrally linked with various subjects both at the level of context and pedagogy.

Navodaya Vidyalayas: No further Navodaya Vidyalayas need be opened. All the existing 261 Navodaya Vidyalayas may be transferred to the state sector for the states to run them as residential centers on The Andhra Pradesh Model. This scheme may be transformed into a Navodaya Vidyalayas program of broad based talent nurturing and pace setting.

16. *National Curriculum Framework in School Education (2000)*

In 1988, the National Council of Educational Research and Training (NCERT) develop 'The National Curriculum for Elementary and Secondary Education: A Framework; in response to The National Policy on Education (NPE), 1986. The revolutionary changes brought about by the information technology necessitated radical changes in the social curriculum to effectively meet with the new challenges. Accordingly, NCERT prepared the 'National Curriculum Framework' in 2000.

Extracts

Early childhood education (ECE)-preparation for primary education (2 years)

This stage of education helps in preparing children for school and constitutes an important element of Early Childhood Care and Education (ECCE).

Elementary education (8 years): Classes I and II, One Language-mother tongue/the regional language, mathematics and art of healthy and productive living. **Classes III to V,** One language-mother tongue/the regional language, environmental studies, mathematics and art healthy and productive living.

Upper primary stage (3 years): Three Languages, mathematics, science and technology, social sciences, work education, art education and health and physical education.

Secondary stage (2 years), Three Languages, Mathematics, Science and technology, Social Science, Work education, Art education and Health and physical education

Curriculum organization at the higher secondary stage: After the 10 years of common program of studies, according to one of the most important recommendations of the Kothari-commission, the curriculum at this stage is to be organized under two streams. However, there is a need to ensure that appropriate linkages between the two are not only maintained but systematically strengthened.

17. *National Curriculum Framework (2005)*

The present revision of NCF was initiated following the statement made by the Hon'ble Minister for Human Resources Development in the Lok Sabha that NCERT should take up such a revision. Accordingly, NCERT set up the National Steering Committee under The Chairmanship of Professor Yashpal. The 21 National Focus Groups, also chaired by renowned scholars and practitioners covered the following major areas.

Recommendations

i.   The national system of education should be strengthened in a pluralistic society.

ii. A renewed effort should be made to implement the three language formula with emphasis on mother-tongue as the medium of instruction.

iii. It recommended that environmental education should become integral part of every subject.

iv. It recommended a paradigm shifts to study social science from the perspective of marginalized groups.

v. It recommended that peace education should form a component of teacher education and the art should comprise a subject at every stage of school education.

vi. The NCF recommended the systematic changes in turn with curriculum reforms.

vii. Agencies and settings offering work opportunities outside the school should be formally recognized.

viii. Health and Physical education are necessary for the overall development of learners through health and physical education programs.

ix. Reducing the curriculum load based on insight provided in "Learning without Burden".

18. *National Knowledge Commission (2005)*

National knowledge Commission is an Indian think-tank charged with considering possible policies that might sharper India's comparative advantage in the knowledge-intensive service sectors. It was constituted on 13 June 2005, by the Prime Minister of India Dr. Manmohan Singh, under the Chairmanship of Sam Pitroda.

Recommendations

Access to knowledge: Certain issues that are being examined in the context by the NKC are: Right to Education, Language, Translation, Libraries, Networks and Portals.

Knowledge concepts: NKC's concern with many aspects of the Indian education system covers: school education, vocational education, higher education, medical education, legal education, management education, engineering education, open and distance education, open educational resources, more talented students in math's & science, more quality PhD's.

Creation of knowledge: India must examine issues such as: science and technology, legal framework for public funded research, intellectual property rights, innovation and entrepreneurship.

Knowledge applications: Knowledge can be productively applied to promote technical change and facilitate reliable and regular flow of information. Knowledge can be very effectively applied for the betterment of the rural poor like traditional knowledge, agriculture and enhancing quality of Life

Delivery of services: E- Governance is one of the ways in which citizens can be empowered to increase transparency of government functioning, leading to greater efficiency and productivity.

MAJOR FINDINGS OF THE ABOVE SECTION

It is quite clear that the base of the contemporary structure of education in India has originated in 1835. Earlier, there was informal and non-formal education in most parts of India. The Englishmen streamlined the system in order to standardize the education system in India. There were various education commissions which formulated the policies and programmes for the upliftment of whole educational system throughout the country. The main aim of these committees, commissions and reports was to provide for education for everyone and to universalize the free and compulsory elementary education with basic facilities, proper training of teachers, facilities for adult education, village libraries and to promote girl education.

After independence the whole system of education was revolutionized throughout the country. The aim of these commissions, Committee report and acts enhanced from primary to university level in an educationally backwards state where muslin's do not pay proper attention towards modern education. It is evident from fact that in 1961, the state was having 11.03%literacy rate while the same rate is 68.74% now. The state has been geographically, politically, socially, economically, topographical and linguistically different from the rest of the country, but these policies have been fruitful for enhancement of literacy rate in J&K, but still J&K is lagging behind with 68.74% from the national average literacy rate which is 74.04% and at the same time the South-Kashmir is lacking with an average of 63.55% which is less than the state average. From the above, it clear that J&K is still struggling to achieve the national literacy rate. In general J&K has low literacy rate but particular South Kashmir is far behind the state level.

SECTION C

CAUSES BEHIND THE GROWTH OF PRIVATE INSTITUTIONS

The tables which follow this paragraph will help us better understand the present educational situation in the South Kashmir region. For this we have given the complete information about the distribution of the public and private schools, the infrastructural and other facilities available in these schools. It also compares the accountability of these schools and also shows the statistics about the inspections and checking's done by the authorities to maintain the standards in these schools. This will help us better understand the reasons behind the growth of the private institutions.

Table No. 4.18: Shows the distribution of public and private schools of South Kashmir

Year	Public/Private schools	Total number of schools	Total enrolment	%age of growth of schools in numbers	%age of growth in enrolment
1951	Public	446	25294	0	0
	Private	35	3528	0	0
1961	Public	718	44458	60.98	75.76
	Private	46	5551	31.42	57.34
1971	Public	939	62946	30.77	41.58
	Private	55	7764	19.56	39.86
1981	Public	1254	94251	33.54	49.73
	Private	128	20325	132.72	161.79
1991	Public	1493	133366	19.05	41.50
	Private	200	34575	56.25	70.11
2001	Public	1914	151376	28.19	13.50
	Private	310	63463	55.00	83.552
2011	Public	3251	242012	69.85	59.87
	Private	622	124017	100.64	95.41
2012	Public	3256	242081	0.15	0.02
	Private	649	132048	4.34	6.47
2013	Public	3254	240320	-0.06	-0.72
	Private	657	134543	1.23	1.88

The above table shows the statistics about the public and private schools in South Kashmir region. We can see a gradual growth in both the number of school as well as the enrolment indicating a good educational environment in the region. We can observe from the table that the no of public schools and the enrolment in these schools has decreased in the year 2012-13. We can see a remarkable growth in the number as well as enrolment of students in the private schools in the decade 2001-2011. Also the private schools have more number of students per school compared to the public schools.

Table No. 4.19: Shows the infra-structural facilities in public and private schools of South Kashmir

Infrastructure		Public institutions	Private institutions
School building	Owner	72%	55%
	Rental	28%	45%
Type of rooms	Adequate	12%	100%
	Inadequate	88%	0%
Drinking water facilities	Yes	65%	100%
	No	35%	0%
Availability of playground	Yes	21%	87%
	No	79%	13%
Availability of transport facilities	Yes	0%	37%
	No	100%	63%
Availability of library	Yes	19%	92%
	No	81%	8%
Facility of electricity	Yes	27%	100%
	No	73%	0%
Fencing of school	Yes	61%	100%
	No	39%	0%

The above table shows the infrastructural facilities available in the schools both private and public in the South Kashmir region. The table shows that the private schools fare much better in providing the basic infrastructural facilities required for the education of the students as compared to the public schools.

Table No. 4.20: Shows the inspection and supervision in public and private schools of South Kashmir

Inspections and supervision		Public institutions	Private institutions
Inspection by officers from education department	Regular	0%	0%
	Rare	70%	100%
	Not at all	30%	0%
Does the inspection help in the improvement of education	Yes	2%	26%
	No	98%	74%

The above table shows the statistics about the inspection and supervision of the public and private institutions in the South Kashmir region by the education department.

Table No. 4.21: Shows the accountability in public and private schools of South Kashmir

Accountability		Public institutions	Private institutions
System of accountability	Yes	0%	100%
	No	100%	0%
Nature of accountability	Strict check of regularity and punctuality	0%	100%
	Regular monitoring of teachers &students progress	0%	100%
	Implementation of hire & fire policy	0%	100%
	Feedback from the parents	0%	100%

The above table shows the statistics about the accountability of the public and private institutions in the South Kashmir region. We can observe that the private institutions fare much better than the public institutions in this aspect.

Table No. 4.22: Shows the academic information in public and private schools of South Kashmir

Academic information		Public institutions	Private institutions
Satisfied with the teaching in the school	Yes	100%	100%
	No	0%	0%
Staff fully trained	Yes	83%	41%
	No	17%	59%
Academic nature of the students	Average	23%	72%
	Below average	77%	28%
	Above average	0%	0%
Response of the parents to the report	Poor	85%	0%
	Satisfactory	0%	100%
	No response	15%	0%
Regular checking of note books by teachers	Yes	86%	100%
	No	14%	0%
Maintaining of dairy by the teacher	Yes	0%	95%
	No	100%	5%
Co-curricular activities in the school	Yes	20%	100%
	No	80%	0%
Community support towards the school	Encouraging	0%	85%
	No support	100%	15%
Availability of teaching learning material	Adequate	0%	100%
	Inadequate	100%	0%
Availability of copy of curriculum	Yes	0%	100%
	No	100%	0%
Headmasters takes period	Yes	91%	35%
	No	9%	65%
Age of headmasters	35-50Years	37%	62%
	50 and Above	73%	38%

The above table gives us a general overview of the situation of teaching in the schools in the South Kashmir region. We can see that there are some things which are basically lacking in the government schools like there is no interaction with the parents, regular checking of notebooks, co-curricular activities and others.

The answers given to the questionnaires by the headmasters of both public and private institutions regarding the growth of private institutions and the researcher's opinion on it:

1. The average age of the headmasters of the public institutions is around 50 to 60 years and that of the headmasters of the private institutions is 35 to 65 years. Usually the headmasters of private institutions are the teachers, headmasters, and principals who retire from the public services, experienced and licensed, and they are preferred because of their experience and hence reappointed to use their experience. Usually the headmasters of public institutions have lesser qualifications than their counterparts in the private sector but at the same time they are highly trained, sometimes better than their peers in the private sector. These headmasters who show poor results while working in the public institutions show much better results while joining the private institutions. The reason behind this being the facilities, accountability, parental care, working under the threat of being fired out which are all a part and parcel of this sector. Also one more reason being that some of the headmasters of these private institutions are on the board of the managing committee of the institutions, have a share in these institutions.

2. One more interesting feature is that in these private institutions most of the headmasters are males, the reason for this being that the managing committee prefers males to females in order to execute the authority delegated on them by the committee.

3. A majority of these public institutions are more than twenty years old and housed in rented buildings and if in case the school has its own building it is neither renovated nor expanded thus portraying a very sad state of affair among its clientele whereas the private institutions which are housed in rented buildings are spacious, furnished and regularly-taken care .

4. The public institutions have their medium of instruction as Urdu which blocks the chances of competition at the later stages of education and also hampers the results of the wards during external examinations.

5. Most of the times even the curriculum in these public institutions is transacted through the mother tongue, Kashmiri, contrary to the private institutions where the curriculum is mainly transacted either in Urdu or English.

6. Also the unchecked mushrooming of these private institutions around the public institutions made them easily accessible to the students who live in the surroundings making them preferable when compared to the public institutions.

7. Also in the public institutions there is an annual decrease in the enrolment but the same is increasing in the private institution. This is due to the better results, attractive building, easy access and English as the medium of instruction these private institutions.

8. While Most of the public school children receive the incentives from the public in the form of uniform, text books which are not available for the private institutions. In spite of these incentives and free education parents are not lured towards public institutions but prefer to invest for better education of children by sending them to private institutions.

9. It is observed that it only the people who belong to the lowest class of the society and have meager income of Rs 1000 to 2000 per month who have no other choice than to send their children to the public institutions. Whereas the middle and the upper classes of the society prefer to get their wards educated in the private institutions. A typical example in this regard is as soon as their financial position improves the parent whose child is reading in public school will immediately get him discharged from the public school and admit him/her in the private school.

10. The main competitors of these private institutions are not the public institutions, but the private institutions in turn compete with one another by investing money and working hard to improve upon the quality of education.

11. The teacher pupil ratio in the public institutions is 1:10 whereas it is in the range of 1:25 to 1:30in the private institutions. But still there is no improvement in the quality of education in the public institutions despite the ratio being ideal for the teaching- learning process. The main factors which are responsible for this are the lack of dedication and commitment to the job.

12. Having the pre-primary classes in public institutions is a dream while it is mandatory in all the private institutions to have the preprimary classes.

13. There are no administrative and academic inspections for the private institutions by the department or statutory bodies, while there is a system in place for the public Institutions for inspections, they are rarely carried out. The private institutions usually have their own internal system of evaluating their processes where every teacher is accountable to the headmaster and he in turn is answerable to the managing committee, with strict adherence to the hire and fire policy. At the same time, there is a complete lack of accountability in the Public institutions where sometimes the performance levels are very bad.

14. While the public schools are still working in unhygienic and miserable conditions where even basic facilities like drinking water, toilet facilities, proper furniture for teachers and children, playground and electricity are not available for most of the time, the private institutions fare much better in these aspects which makes it attractive for the parents to send them to these institutions which is helping them increase their enrolment and also leading to the closure of many public schools.

15. The headmasters of the public institutions are usually pre occupied with class work thereby sparing no time for administration and maintenance of the school whereas in the private institutions the headmasters rarely take the class and are continuously supervising the administrative aspects, academic transactions, parent meetings and general improvement of the school.

16. As compared to the children of public institutions, the children in the private institutions are above average academically and they are regularly being supported academically in the school and at home.

17. The private institutions which have a well-established system of co-curricular activities take care of all the developmental aspects of the children whereas in the public institutions the mental development is only stressed upon and other aspects like physical, emotional, aesthetic and spiritual aspects are totally ignored.

18. There are no teacher guide books in both the private and public institutions to guide the teacher on how to teach, the result of which is that every teacher has developed his/her own methodology in teaching-learning transactions which are not in accordance with the methodology recommended by the experts at the state and national level.

19. When asked for suggestions for the improvement of the state of affairs in their institutions, most of the headmasters of the public institutions suggested inclusion of the accountability, provision of requisite facilities, regular inspections and supervisions for improvement of the education standards in their institutions while most of the headmasters of the private institutions suggested financial support from the public, training for the teachers ,a better pay scale and streamlining of the accountability in their institutions.

Answers to the questionnaire exclusively prepared for the headmasters of private sector schools:

1. The headmasters replied that the reason why these institutions were opened is to take the quality education to the door steps of the people.

2. The fee received from the students are quite enough to equip the school with the requisite facilities, but the teachers who are the main back bone of these educational institutions are not satisfied with the salary they are receiving which clearly indicates that these institutions have clear motives of commercial benefits. These Institutions are free to decide the fee structure for their institutions with no check from any agency, thus these institutions qualify for being tuition shops than educational centers.

3. Some of the private institutions admit students who are very poor, orphans and handicaps in their school and teach them without charging any fee. The number of students who are admitted in this manner in the private institutions is very negligible but this is positive sign and needs encouragement from the government.

The headmasters of both the public and private institutions are of the same opinion that presently there is better education provided in the private institutions, so the numbers of public institutions are declining and the private institutions are flourishing. It is a matter of grave public concern that the very persons who are looking after the public system have such opinions against their institutions which mandate an immediate attention at all the levels of hierarchy.

Questions specifically posed to the parents of the children studying in the in public institutions:

1. The main reason for sending the children to the public institutions appeared to be poverty. The parents also expressed the desire that if they had a better financial position they have afforded a better quality of education for the children thereby covertly expressing their dissatisfaction with the quality of education offered in the public schools.

2. The parents were also mostly unaware about the quality and better education offered by the private institutions but they simply wanted to send their wards there due to the craze and the public image associated with them.

Questions specially posed to the parents of the children who are studying in private institutions:

1. Almost all the parents expressed their displeasure with the public institutions because of the lack of facilities, lack of commitment among the teachers, unattractive environment, the medium of education and the lack of accountability. The same views are prevailing in the whole society as such and make the education in the public schools very unattractive.

2. The above views are also largely shared by most of the teachers who also favor the private institutions since they are attractive, are performing better, have better facilities with accountability in most of the aspects and have English as the medium of instruction. At the other end of the spectrum there are some teachers who have blamed the private institutions for commercializing the education sector working as tuition shops rather than centers of education, having untrained teachers and exploiting the peoples craze for better quality of education.

The above opinions expressed by the parent's shows that the public system has failed in respect to the private educational institutions.

Opinion of the researcher on the answers given to the questionnaires by the parents whose wards are studying in public and private institutions:

1. The parents who have enrolled their children in the public institutions are mostly illiterate and usually don't take care of the study needs of the children at home thus leaving them exclusively at the mercy of the teachers in these institutions. Because of their illiteracy these parents are not able to differentiate between mere education and better or quality education. Also, they are not able to foresee the future of the child in view of the existing knowledge explosion. The situation is completely different in case of the parents who have enrolled their children in the private institutions with most of them taking a lot of interest in the education of their children and also because most of them are educated they are well aware of the investment to be made in the education of their children.

2. Most of the parents whose children are enrolled in the public institutions are working in the unorganized sector working from dawn to dusk to earn a living for their family leaving them with no time to spare for the educational care of their children, which ultimately results in the poor academic performance by these children, while the case is much better in parents who have enrolled their wards in the private institutions. Most of them are employees and businessmen and are much better financially and also have time to concentrate on the education of their children.

3. Most of the children who attend the children attending the public schools do so basing their selection of school on the proximity of the school to their home, most of them attending the school within 1 km radius of their homes, while the children who go to the private institutions base their selection on the basis of other factors like the type of education and other facilities offered in those schools.

4. The mother tongue of most of the students is Kashmiri and the parents and children who are reading in public institutions mainly speak and transact in their mother tongue which is usually prohibited in private institutions. This leads to problems when a child who comes from a public school background and tries to interact with a child from a private school. They are placed at an unfair disadvantage as they don't have the necessary skills to transact in a different foreign language also, the parents of the

wards who are reading in private institutions restrict their children from speaking in their mother tongue and are thrilled to use a language other than the mother tongue, which is an irony and completely in contrast to the education policy.

5. Almost all of the public institutions have Urdu as their medium of instruction, which acts as a barrier to the student when he goes for higher education which is mostly done in English, here the students from the private schools have an advantage as their whole education is done in English which helps them to compete with their peers better in the latter stages of their education.

6. The average monthly income of the parents who send their children to the public schools is around Rs.1000-2000 and with this income it is very difficult to make their ends meet leave alone giving proper nutritious meals and proper education. Also since the income of the families is so less they would want more number of hands earning for their family and this engage their children in some work to supplement their income, which adversely affects the education of their children. The situation is much better in case of the children studying in the private institutions and is able to focus better on their education.

7. The children who study in the public institutions get free text books and uniform so the parents don't incur much expenditure on their education and thus are non-serious and don't show any authority in monitoring the education of their children whereas the parents whose children study in the private institutions invest substantial amount on the education of their children and thus obligated to care more about the quality of the education their children are receiving. This also makes the school administration and teachers to be on their toes which are not the case with the public schools whereas the parents neither have the time nor the resources to care about the school.

8. The parents whose children are studying in the private institutions make it a point to attend the parent teacher meetings leaving all their other assignments and discuss their wards academic performance and give the necessary suggestions for the betterment of the school. These meetings also help the parents to keep a track of the behavior changes in their wards and take necessary care whereas the above care is totally lacking in the case of the children of public institutions.

9. The parents of the children who are studying in the public institutions are hardly able to make their ends meet thus there is no question of them sparing money for a private tutor leaving the children's education completely to the mercy of whatever is taught in the schools, in contrast to this the parents of children who study in the private schools sometimes spend upwards of Rs.3000 on private coaching. Usually this extra coaching helps them better their performance of children which is used as money making machine by the owners of these private institutions.

Data obtained from the interviews with the Director School Education, Joint Director School Education, Chief Education Officers and Zonal Education Officers of South Kashmir on:

a. Reasons for closure of public institutions

1. No proper planning and research done while establishing these public institutions and mushrooming of the private institutions around the public institutions.
2. Lack of interest among the students to continue in the public institutions and also due to the migration of families from one to other due to work or other reasons.
3. Lack of administrative gearing up at regular intervals.

b. Reasons for decline in the enrolment of children in public institutions

1. Inadequate infra structural facilities.
2. Lack of dedication and commitment of teachers and also uneven distribution.
3. Poor performance of the children coming out of these institutions.
4. Lack of accountability at any level in the system
5. The primary medium of instruction in most schools being Urdu.

c. Reasons for mushroom growth of private institutions

1. Recognition granted in violation of public rules.
2. Every person whether professional or non-professional in the fray of opening the school.
3. Commercialization of education.
4. No accountability towards public.
5. Parents becoming more aspiration for their children.
6. Availability of a large number of teachers due to the large number of unemployed

youth usually among females who are waiting to jump and grab the opportunity.

7. Social stigma against the public institutions which has transformed into a craze for the private schools.

d. How is mushroom growth of private institutions influencing the functioning of public institutions?

1. Public institutions receiving below average students thereby frustrating the teachers.
2. Better quality of education is provided at the door steps of the parents so they prefer private institutions to public institutions leaving the public institutions high and dry.
3. Some private institutions with lees fee structure have attracting the parents of lower class families who think that private schools are much better.
4. The families whose financial position improves over a period of time, withdraws his child from the public school and puts him or her in the private school.
5. Due to poor results in the examination, wrong signals are carried to the society thus the society also starts disowning the public system of education.

e. What can be done to check the growth of private institutions?

1. By improving the quality of education in the public institutions
2. By implementing uniform code of conduct for all the institutions.
3. Making the institutions fully accountable to the public.
4. Strict recognition policy, not to allow any private school in close vicinity of public school.
5. Private institutions to be brought under the ambit of inspections and supervisions by educational authorities.

Opinion of the researcher on the views of the officers to the interview schedules:

1. The officers of the education department have themselves said that a number of public institutions have closed due to lack of attention towards these institutions. They also agreed that the growth of the private institutions due to managed recognition have thrown the public institutions into oblivion. The government has made no efforts at all to revive these institutions and put in efforts to stop the closure of these institutions. It is also a reality that the public institutions perform poorly as compared to private institutions .The lack of accountability, lack of infra structural

facilities, lack of commitment of teachers, Urdu as medium of instruction are some of the impediments in improving the quality of education in these institutions.

2. In the rapid growth and mushrooming of these private institutions the authorities have played a significant role. The dominance of the private schools is now a reality which we can't escape; they are substantiating the public efforts in educating the people so these institutions need to be streamlined with a check by the public. Also the public institutions have lost the credibility and the support of the society which is hard to win back.

3. The officers have also accepted the fact that these private schools have no public control and are free to exploit the parents on one hand and the teachers on the other.

4. The officers have also admitted that they have no time to spare for visits to these institutions, result being that these institutions go Scot free.

5. The officers have also shown concern about the children of under privileged, but there are no significant measures being taken for their education by the government.

MAJOR FINDINGS OF THE ABOVE SECTION

It has been found that the private schools fare much better in providing the basic infrastructural facilities required for the education of the students as compared to the public schools like drinking water, playground, library, transport etc. The main things which are basically lacking in the government schools are no interaction with the parents, regular checking of notebooks, maintaining of dairy by the teacher co-curricular activities and others.

The reason behind this being the facilities, accountability, parental care, working under the threat of being fired out which are all a part and parcel of private sector. While most of the public school children receive the incentives from the public in the form of uniform, text books which are not available for the private institutions. It is observed that it only the people who belong to the lowest class of the society and have meager income of Rs 1000 to 2000 per month who have no other choice than to send their children to the public institutions. Whereas middle and upper class people of the society prefer to get their wards educated in the private institutions.

It was found that the fee received from the students are quite enough to equip the school with the requisite facilities, but the teachers who are the main back bone of these educational institutions are not satisfied with the salary they are receiving which clearly indicates that these institutions have clear motives of commercial benefits. The parents whose children are studying in the private institutions make it a point to attend the parent teacher meetings leaving all their other assignments and discuss their wards academic performance and give the necessary suggestions for the betterment of the school. These meetings also help the parents to keep a track of the behavior changes in their wards and take necessary care whereas the above care is totally lacking in the case of the children of public institutions.

The investigator also found that most of the teachers, who in their individual capacity also favor the private institutions since they are attractive, are performing better, have better facilities with accountability in most of the aspects and have English as the medium of instruction. At the other end of the spectrum there are some teachers who have blamed the private institutions for commercializing the education sector working as tuition shops rather than centers of education, having untrained teachers and exploiting the peoples craze for better quality of education. The officers of the education department have themselves said that a number of public institutions have closed due to lack of attention towards this institutions.

SECTION – D

COMMONALITY AND DIFFERENCE IN THE SYLLABUS PRESCRIBED BY THE PUBLIC AND PRIVATE INSTITUTIONS

In this section, it is highlighted that there are two types of schools selected, namely private and public schools, to study the commonalities and also the differences in the syllabus prescribed in various schools of South Kashmir. While collecting and analyzing the data, it has been found that there is only a single series/publication of books (tulip series) in all the government schools throughout the valley of Kashmir and the quality and standard of printing is neither good nor are these books attractive/good looking. At the same time the situation in the private schools in this aspect is wholly different. These schools have a number of series/publications and publishers but the fact remains that the gist of all the series of books is the same in private schools. The books of private schools are much more attractive, good looking and qualitative in terms of material used. Besides, there are various commonalities and differences in the syllabus prescribed by various private and public schools of south Kashmir. The data for this purpose has been collected with the help of a questionnaire and the collected data has been analyzed and represented in the below tabulation form:

Table No. 4.23: Showing the commonalities and differences in the syllabus prescribed by the public and private institutions from 1st to 2nd standard

Items	Public schools	Private schools
Total number of subjects taught	(Four) English, Urdu, Math & Kashmiri	(Nine) English, Kashmiri, Urdu, Math's, Science, Drawing, EVS, G. K ,Computer
Medium of instruction	Urdu and English	Urdu and English
Syllabus framing body	Jammu Kashmir Board of School Education	Own body to design syllabus and amendments can be made easily, whenever needed.
Total time period for the completion of the prescribed syllabus	8-9 months	8-9 months
School timing	• 10 am to 4 pm (Winter) • 9 am to 3pm (Summer)	• 10am – 4pm (Winter) • 9am -3pm (Summer)
Educational objectives/instructional objectives	Development of 3R's	• Development of 3R's • Overall development of personality • Skill enhancement • Efficacy in communication
Provision of co-curricular activities	Negligible	• Spacious time and arrangements for such activities
Method of teaching	• Old traditional • Lecture method • Drill method	• Lecture Method • Play way method • Project method • Problem solving method
System of examination & evaluation	• Oral examination • Summative evaluation • Rare provision to provide progress report • Poor coordination between parents and teachers	• Oral & written Examinations • Formative as well as summative evaluation • Suitable provision to provide progress report throughout the session • Qualitative coordination as well as cooperative between parents and teachers
Teaching aids	• Classical Visual aids like black board, white board, charts etc.	• Modern A/V aids like Projectors, electronic gadgets, LCD's. They also use Classical Visual aids like black board, white board, charts etc.

The above table shows that the numbers of subjects taught in private schools are more than that of public schools. There are nine subjects taught in private schools whereas the public schools have only four subjects at this stage. The above table also shows that schools are providing information/education as per the needs and demands of society, whereas on the other hand the public schools are concentrating only on languages and arithmetic at this level. They are far behind in providing the very kind of education which is the need of the hour. So, it is crystal clear that the public schools are much more advanced and are geared up to provide qualitative as well as quantitative education in comparison to a public school. From the above, we can easily say that the difference is the number of subjects taught is what develops the mental faculties/abilities of a student in private school at early stage and polish their talent in terms of art and creatively. Whereas, the same is lacking in public schools which is the main reason that the students of the said schools are handicapped in terms of modern and current needs and demands of the society.

So far as medium of instruction is concerned, the above table shows that the medium of instruction is same in both the public as well as private schools, where Urdu and English is used as a medium of instruction.

From the above table it is evident that there are separate syllabus framing bodies for both the public and private schools. Jammu Kashmir Board of School Education is designing/framing and regulating body for the syllabus of public schools whereas, private school are having there autonomous syllabus designing /framing and regulating bodies. They can revise/amend/change the syllabus as per the demand of the society and need of the hour. At the same time the situation in a public school is different i.e. they cannot change/amend or revise the syllabus so quickly. This is the main reason why they are lagging behind in providing the latest information to the nook and corner of the society, whereas private sector is providing door to door service in terms latest education/information and technology.

The above table reveals that the total duration of time for the completion of syllabus in both public as well as private school is some i.e. 8-9 months as both sectors lie under the umbrella of Jammu Kashmir Board of School Education. Undoubtedly, private schools are having their own syllabus but they must follow the instruction of Jammu Kashmir Board of

School Education. When we compare the no. of gazetted holidays, the public schools have much more holidays as compared to private school. Form this point it is crystal clear that the no. of working days get enhanced or increased in private schools, which maintains their quality and productivity.

From, the above table it is quite clear that the school timing is same in both the sectors i.e. 10am to 4pm during winters. While as, this timing gets changed during summers and starts from 9am up to 3pm. In this regard both the sectors are following the instruction from the director, directorate of school education, Kashmir.

So far as the educational objectives/educational instructions are concerned, the above table reflects that there is a big difference in both public &private sectors of education regarding the educational objectives. The main educational objectives of public schools are development of 3R's i.e. reading, writing and arithmetic. On the other hand the environment is totally different in private school. The private schools have a plethora of educational objectives like development of 3R's i.e. reading, writing and arithmetic, overall development of personality like, physical, mental, social emotional etc, skill enhancement and efficiency in communication. So it is quite clear that private schools are providing multi-dimensional development of a child as compared to the public schools. This is the reason that the foundation or we can say plinth of private school students is very strong in academic and other life related activities as compared to those students who are enrolled in public schools.

The above table shows that there is negligible provision for co-curricular activities in public schools at this stage but, at the same time the same thing is in present in private schools quantitatively as well as qualitatively.

In private schools, the spacious time and arrangements are made for the co-curricular and extra-curricular activities, which in the long run provide a solid environment for the teaching and learning process. The students of these schools learn much more things and enjoy the environment of education as much as they can but the same thing is lacking in the public schools.

The table also reflects that the method of teaching is also a different in both private and public school at this level. The public schools are using old traditional method, lecture method and to some extant drill method, whereas, in private school, it is quite different. They are using number of different teaching methods, modern as well as traditional like lecture method play way method project problem solving method etc. These methods are more professional and technical methods of teaching and through these methods, the child can enjoy the learning environment as much as possible without feeling burden. With the help of project method, play way method and problem solving method the mental, cognitive and emotional development of the children is possible very early. We can simply say that the overall development of education is the result of the said methods of teaching. Whereas, at the same time these methods are almost absent in public schools. That is the reason why the development is delayed.

So far as the system of examination and evaluation is concerned, the above table shows that there is great diversity in both public and private schools in this aspect. The examination system is almost oral at these stages. There is a negligible provision for written examinations at the above said stages. These schools have the summative systems of evaluation i.e. evaluation only once in a session (at the end of the year). In these schools there is no provision to provide students report and they also do not have the teacher parent meetings. Whereas at the same time there is a formative kind of examination and evaluation system in private schools at this stage. Private schools make quantitative arrangements for both oral and written examination throughout the year. They divide their examination and evaluation into various fragments like unit exams which removes the burden from the shoulders of the students. There is a suitable arrangement to provide program reports of students not only at the end of the year but throughout the year. They have also environment of good and qualitative meetings with parents. These meetings give a plethora of new ideas to the teachers and parents and managing authorities of the school. When we compare the same thing with the public sector at this stage it is crystal clear that the public sector is far behind than that of private sector, qualitatively as well as quantitatively.

The above table also shows that the aids which are used in public schools are classical such as black boards/ while board charts etc. which have been in use from a long time. Whereas there is a quite contrasting situation prevalent in the private schools. Private schools are using various old as well as new teaching aids. Private schools are using various old as well as new teaching aids like black board, white charts, maps, projectors, electronic gadgets,

LCD's etc. So it is clear from the above that public schools are lacking in such facilities and the result of that is unawareness about the modern means of education and so on. Private school with their modern means of teaching aids shows better performance as compared to that of public schools.

Table No. 4.24: Showing the commonalities and difference in the syllabus prescribed by the public and private institutions from 3rd- 5th standard

Items	Public schools	Private schools
No of subjects	(Five) English, Urdu, Math's, EVS & Kashmiri	(Nine) English, Kashmiri, Urdu, Math's, Science, Drawing, Social Science, G.K ,Computer
Medium of instruction	Kashmiri, Urdu and English	Kashmiri, Urdu and English
Syllabus framing body	Jammu Kashmir Board of School Education	Own body to design syllabus and amendments can be made easily, when ever needed.
Total duration for the completion of the prescribed syllabus	8-9 months	8-9 months
School timing	• 10 am to 4 pm (Winter) • 9 am to 3pm (Summer)	• 10am – 4pm (Winter) • 9am -3pm (Summer)
Educational objectives/instructional objectives	Development of 3R's and Language	• Development of Language • Overall development of personality • Skill enhancement • Efficacy in communication
Provision of co-curricular activities	Negligible	• Spacious time and arrangements for such activities
Method of teaching	• Old traditional • Lecture method • Drill method	• Lecture Method • Project method • Problem solving method
System of examination & evaluation	• Oral and written examination • Summative evaluation • Rare provision to provide progress report • Poor coordination between parents and teachers	• written Examinations • Formative as well as summative evaluation • Suitable provision to provide progress report throughout the session • Qualitative coordination as well as cooperative between parents and teachers
Teaching aids	• Classical Visual aids like black board, white board, charts etc.	• Modern A/V aids like Projectors, electronic gadgets, LCD's. They also use Classical Visual aids like black board, white board, charts etc.

The above table shows that that the number of subjects in private schools is more than that of public schools. There are nine subjects in private schools whereas the public schools are only having five subjects at this stage. This is the first juncture in public schools where environmental studies starts. The above table also shows that private schools are given that information/education as per the requirements and demands of people whereas on the other hand the public schools lack in providing the same at this level. Thus it is obvious that the public schools are to a large extent sophisticated to endow the students with qualitative as well as quantitative education as compared to public school.

From the above table, we can easily say that this is the fundamental reason which expands the mental faculties/abilities of the students in private school at a very nascent age and shines their thinking skills in terms of talent and innovation. The same is deficient in public schools, the students of which are handicapped in conditions of modern and up to date requirements and demands of the society.

So far as medium of instruction is concerned, the above table shows that the medium of instruction is the same in both the public as well as private schools. Both the public and private schools are using Urdu and English as medium of instruction. But the main focus of private schools is towards English and majority of them use it as their medium of instruction.

From the above table it is palpable that there are different syllabus framing bodies of both the public and private school. Jammu Kashmir Board of School Education is designing/framing and regulating the syllabus of public schools whereas, private school are having their own independent syllabus designing /framing and regulating body. They can improve/amend/modify the syllabus as per the demands of the society and need of the hour. At the same time public school are having entirely diverse situation i.e. they cannot modify/improve or revise the syllabus so quickly. This is the main reason why they fail to provide for the best and latest information to the nook and corner of the society, whereas private sector is providing door to door service in terms of most recent education/information and technology.

The above table reveals that the total duration of time for the completion of syllabus in both public as well as private school is the same i.e. 8-9 months as both sectors lies underneath the sunshade of J&K BOSE. Unquestionably, private schools are having their own syllabus but they must tag on the instruction of Jammu Kashmir Board of School Education. When we match up to the no. of public holidays, public schools have some additional holidays as compared to private school. Form this end it is clear that the no. of functioning days get enhanced or increased in private schools, which maintains their excellence and output.

From, the above table it is fairly obvious that the school timing is same in both the sectors i.e. 10am to 4pm during winters. Whereas, this timing gets altered in summers and starts from 9am up to 3pm. In this regard both the sectors are operating subsequent to the instructions from the director directorate of school education, Kashmir.

So far as the educational objectives/educational instructions are concerned, the above table reflects that there is a gigantic dissimilarity in both public &private sectors of education concerning the educational objectives. The main educational objectives of public schools are development of 3R's i.e. reading, writing and arithmetic. On the other hand the atmosphere is completely different in private school. The private schools different educational objectives like development of 3R's i.e. reading, writing and arithmetic, overall development of personality like, physical, mental, social emotional etc, skill enhancement and efficiency in communication. So it is fairly obvious that private schools are providing multi-dimensional maturity of a child as compared to the public schools. This is the main reason why the base of the private school students is very strong in academic and other life related behavior as compared to those students who enrolled in public schools.

The above table also shows that there is an insignificant provision for co-curricular activities in public schools at this stage but, at the same time the similar item is in present in private schools quantitatively as well as qualitatively.

In private schools, the spacious time and planning are ready for the co-curricular and extra-curricular behavior, which in the long run supply a solid atmosphere for the teaching learning process. The students of these schools learn much more things and enjoy the environment of education as much as they can but the same thing is lacking in the public schools.

The table also reflects that the method of teaching is also a different in both private and public school at this level. The public schools have been teaching through the means of aged long-established method, lecture method and to some extant drill method, whereas, in private school, it is quite different. They are using number of teaching methods, contemporary as well as customary like lecture method, play way method, project problem solving method etc. These methods are almost professional and technical methods of teaching. Through these methods, the child can learn in an environment which is most productive for learning. With the help of project method, play way method and problem solving method the child, mental, cognitive and emotional development is possible very early. We can simply say that the on the whole, advancement of education is the product of the said methods of teaching. Whereas at the same time these methods are more or less absent in public schools. That is why their progress is postponed.

So far as the system of assessment and evaluation is concerned from above table shows that there is enormous diversity in both public and private schools concerning the said things in public schools, the examination system is written as well as oral at these stages. These schools are having the summative systems of evaluation i.e. evaluation only once in a session (at the end of the year). In these schools provisions are still trying to make provisions to provide students' progress report they also miss the provision for teacher parent meetings. Whereas at the same time there is a formative kind of examination and evaluation system in private schools at this stage. Private schools made quantitative arrangements for both oral and written examination throughout the year. They divide their examination and evaluation into various fragments like unit exams which removes the burden from the shoulders of the students. There is a suitable arrangement to provide program reports of students not only at the end of the year but throughout the year. They also have qualitative meetings with parents. This gave plethora new ideas of to the teachers and parents and managing authorities of the school. When we compare the same thing with the public sector at this stage it is that the public sector is lagging behind that of private sector, qualitatively as well as quantitatively.

The above table also shows that there are traditional teachings aids which are used in public schools such as black boards/ while board charts etc. from a long time, whereas, it is reasonably contrast in private schools. Private schools are using a variety of old as well as new teaching aids. Like black board/ white board charts etc. from a long time, whereas, it is totally different in private schools. Private schools are using a mixture of old as well as new teaching aids like black board, white charts, maps, projectors, electronic gadgets, LCD's etc. So it is apparent from the above that public schools are deficient in such facilities and the effect of that is lack of knowledge about the up to date means of education and so on. Private school with their modern means of teaching aids shows better performance and compared to that of public schools.

Table No. 4.25: Showing the commonalities and difference in the syllabus prescribed by the public and private institutions from 6th - 7th

Items	Public schools	Private schools
No of subjects	(Five) English, Urdu, Math's, Social Science & Kashmiri	(Nine) English, Kashmiri, Urdu, Math's, Science, Drawing, Social Science, G.K ,Computer
Medium of instruction	Kashmiri, Urdu and English	Kashmiri, Urdu and English
Syllabus framing body	Jammu Kashmir Board of School Education	Own body to design syllabus and amendments can be made easily, when ever needed.
Total duration for the completion of the prescribed syllabus	8-9 months	8-9 months
School timing	10 am to 4 pm (Winter) 9 am to 3pm (Summer)	• 10am – 4pm (Winter) • 9am -3pm (Summer)
Main focus of syllabus/subjects	Development of Knowledge about the subjects	• Development of Knowledge about the subject • Overall development of personality • Language enhancement, Efficacy and fluency in communication
Provision of co-curricular activities	Rarely	• Different educational tours, picnics and excursions are made time to time for the overall development of students.
Method of teaching	• Old traditional • Lecture method • Drill method	• Lecture Method • Project method • Problem solving method

System of examination & evaluation	• • written Examinations • Summative evaluation • Rare provision to provide progress report • Poor coordination between parents and teachers	• written and practical Examinations • Formative as well as summative evaluation • Suitable provision to provide progress report throughout the session • Qualitative coordination as well as cooperative between parents and teachers.
Teaching aids	• Classical Visual aids like black board, white board, charts etc.	• Modern A/V aids like overhead Projectors, Educational films, electronic gadgets, LCD's. They also use Classical Visual aids like black board, white board, charts etc.

The above table shows that the figures of subjects in private schools are more than that of public schools. There are nine subjects in private schools whereas public school is having six subjects at this stage. The above table also shows that in the private schools the students are given information/education as per the wants and demands of people, on the other hand the public schools are focused just main subjects at this level. They are far-off to supply each and every sort of education as per the need of the hour. So, it is crystal clear that the private schools are to a vast extent advanced to provide qualitative as well as quantitative education as compared to public school.

From the above, we can say that this is the vital reason which develop the cerebral conveniences /abilities of a student in private school at in the early years and grooms their talent in terms of art and creatively. Whereas, the same is not there in public schools. Thus the students of the supposed schools are handicapped in conditions of modern and up to date requirements and demands of the society

So far as medium of instruction is concerned, the above table shows that the medium of instruction is similar in both the school public as well as private. Both the sectors public and private are by means of Urdu and English as medium of instruction. But in private schools the praise goes in goodwill of English language.

From the above table it is manifest that there are separate syllabus framing bodies of both the public and private school Jammu Kashmir Board of School Education is scheming/framing and modifiable the syllabus of public schools whereas private school are having their independent syllabus conniving /framing and amendable body. They can revise/amend/change the syllabus as per the demand of the society and need of the hour. At the same time public school are having entirely diverse situation i.e. they cannot change/amend or revise the syllabus so rapidly. This is the reason that they are absent to provide latest information to the nook and corner of the society, whereas private sector is providing door to door service in terms most recent education/information and technology.

The above table reveals that the total period of time for the completion of syllabus in both public as well as private school is some i.e. 8-9 months as both sectors lies beneath the sun umbrella of Jammu Kashmir Board of School Education. Undoubtedly, private schools are having their own syllabus but they are being obliged to pursue the instruction of JKBOSE. When we measure up the no. of public holidays, the public school is having some extra holidays as compared to private school. Form this point it is crystal clear that the no. of functioning days get enhanced or increased in private schools, which maintains their quality and production.

From, the above table it is reasonably understandable that the school timing is matching in both the sectors i.e. 10am to 4pm during winters. Also, this timing gets altered during summers and starts from 9am up to 3pm. In this regard both the sectors are following the instruction from the director directorate of school education, Kashmir.

So far as the educational objectives/educational instructions are concerned, the above table reflects that there is a full-size variation in both public &private sectors of education concerning the educational objectives. The main educational objectives of public schools are expansion of information about the subject matter; on the other hand the environment is wholly different in private school. The private schools are having plethora of educational objectives like development of reading, writing and arithmetic, overall development of personality like, physical, mental, social emotional etc, skill enrichment and competence in communication. So it is fairly clear that private schools are providing multi-dimensional development of a child as compared to the public schools. This is the main reason behind the private school students are very strong in academic and other life related actions as compared to those students who enrolled in public schools.

The above table shows that there is a slight provision for co-curricular actions in public schools at this stage but, at the same time the same thing is present in private schools quantitatively as well as qualitatively.

In private schools, there is spacious time and arrangements made for the co-curricular and extra-curricular activities, different educational tours, picnics and excursions are made time to time for the general development of students which in the long run provide a solids\ environment for the teaching learning route. The students of these schools are trained much more and enjoy the environment of education as much as they can but the same thing is missing in the public schools.

The table also reflects that the method of teaching is also diverse in both private and public school at this level. The public schools are using old established method, lecture method and to some extant drill method, whereas, in private school, it is quite different. They are using number teaching methods, modern as well as traditional like lecture method project problem solving method etc. these method are more or less professional and technical methods of teaching., through these methods, the child can learn environment as much as possible without feeling burden. With the help of project method and problem solving method the child, mental, cognitive and emotional development is possible very early. We can simply say that the overall development of education is the result of the said methods of teaching. Whereas at the same time these methods are almost absent in public schools. That is why there development is delayed.

So for as the system of assessment and evaluation is concerned, the above table shows that there is an enormous variety in both public and private schools concerning the said things. In the public schools the assessment system is written and practical at these stages. These schools are having the summative systems of evaluation i.e. evaluation only once in a session (at the end of the year). In these schools provisions are still being made to provide students program report, and these schools also lack the arrangements for teacher parent meetings. Whereas at the same time there is a formative kind of examination and evaluation system in private schools at this stage. Private schools make quantitative arrangements for both practical and written examination throughout the year. They divide their assessment and evaluation into various fragments like unit exams which removes the burden from the shoulders of the students. There is a suitable arrangement to provide the progress reports of students not only at the end of the year but throughout the year. They also have the environment of good and qualitative meetings with parents. This gives a plethora of new ideas to the teachers and parents and organization authorities of the school. When we contrast the same thing with the public sector at this stage it is apparent that the public sector is lagging very far than the private sector, both qualitatively as well as quantitatively.

The above table also shows that there are orthodox teachings aids which are being used in public schools such as black boards/ while board charts etc. from a long time, whereas, there is a fair dissimilarity in private schools. Private schools are using various old as well as new teaching aids like black board white charts maps projectors electronic gadgets, LCD's, overhead projectors etc. So it is obvious from the above that public schools are absent in such amenities and the consequence of that is lack of knowledge about the current means of education and so on. Private school which has the most up to date means of teaching aids shows superior performance as compared to that of public schools.

From primary up to 7th standard there is a difference in terms of content, syllabus, educational objectives etc. but from the 8th standard up to higher level there is no difference at all. The syllabus framing body is Jammu Kashmir Board of School Education and the examinations are conducted under the same. All the examinations from class 8th onwards are the core responsibility of the above mentioned board. It is worth mentioning here that the Jammu Kashmir Board of School Education frames syllabus, conduct examinations, evaluation and all the things which are related to the academics and smooth functioning of the schools.

After class 12th different professional/technical/academic whether private or public are under the direct control of different government control boards/Universities which conduct the examination, design and frame syllabus for different courses and classes. So, it is clear from the above that there is no difference in terms of course and course-content etc in private and public schools from class 8th onwards. Undoubtedly, there is plethora of

112

advanced and sophisticated infrastructure in private sector. The supposed schools conduct more co-curricular and extra-curricular activities as compared to public schools. As a result the students of private schools get more exposure and experience as compare to the students of public schools and their talents get boosted.

Also, from the above it is quite clear that there is no difference in terms of course, course-content and the time duration of the course in both the sectors.

MAJOR FINDINGS OF THE ABOVE SECTION

While analysing the data it has been found that there is only a single series of books which are used in all the government schools throughout the valley of Kashmir and the quality and standard of printing is neither healthy nor are these books are attractive/good looking. At the same time the private schools have a different kind of atmosphere in this regard. They have number a number of series/publications and publishers but the fact remains that the gist of all the series of books are the same. The books of private schools are much more attractive, good looking and qualitative in terms of material used. The numbers of subjects taught in private schools are more than that of public schools. The medium of instruction in both the public as well as private schools is the same and they are both using Urdu and English as their medium of instruction. They have different syllabus framing bodies for both the public and private school, Jammu Kashmir Board of School Education is the designing/framing and regulating body of the public schools whereas the private schools are having their own autonomous syllabus designing /framing and regulating body. The total duration of time for the completion of syllabus in both public as well as private school is same i.e. 8-9 months as this is one aspect which is decided by the Jammu Kashmir Board of School Education. When we compare them to the number of holidays the public schools have many more additional holidays as compared to private school. The timings of the schools are same in both the sectors i.e. 10am to 4pm during winters, whereas this timing gets altered during the summer's i.e. 9am up to 3pm. The main educational objectives of public schools are the development of 3R's i.e. reading, writing, arithmetic and gist of the subjects whereas on the other hand that the atmosphere is completely different in private school. The private schools are having plethora of educational objectives which are the development of 3R's i.e. reading, writing and arithmetic, overall development of personality like, physical, mental, social emotional etc, skill enhancement and efficiency in communication. The method of teaching is also a different in both private and public school at this level. In the public schools it is by means of aged long-established method, lecture method and to some extent the drill method, whereas, in private school, it is quite different. They are using a number of teaching methods, contemporary as well as customary like lecture method play way, method project problem solving method etc. In the public schools, the examination system is written in lower primary standard, and it is written as well as oral at the upper primary standard. These schools have the summative systems of evaluation i.e. evaluation only once in a session (at the end of the year) whereas at the same time there is a formative kind of examination and evaluation system in private schools at this stage. Private schools make quantitative arrangements for both oral and written examination throughout the year.

From the 8th standard up to the higher level there is no difference at all between public and private schools. The syllabus framing body is the Jammu Kashmir Board of School Education and examinations are conducted under the same. All the examinations from class 8th onwards are the core responsibility of the above mentioned board. It is worth mentioning here that the Jammu Kashmir Board of School Education frames the syllabus, conducts examinations, evaluation and all the things which are related to the academics and smooth functioning of the schools. After class 12th different professional/technical/ academic institutes whether private or public are under the direct control of different government control boards/Universities which conduct the examination, design and frame syllabus for different courses and classes. So, it is clear from the above that there is no difference in terms of course and course-content etc. in private and public schools from class 8th onwards.

SECTION – E

SEX-WISE AND RURAL-URBAN LITERACY GROWTH OF SOUTH KASHMIR

The first attempt to take a census in the state of Jammu and Kashmir was made in the year 1873. The results of which, however were not much satisfactory. In 1891 and 1901 regular census was conducted. After that, the census operations, which were in complete conformity with principles and instructions emanating from the Government of India, were held in 1911 to 1941. In 1951, the conditions in the state were not conductive for conducting the census. In 1961, 1971 and 1981 the censuses were taken as a part of the census of India. No census was conducted during 1991 due to administrative difficulties which can mainly be attributed to the problem of militancy being at its peak during this period which made the normal running of administrative functions difficult. The whole of the Kashmir valley was witness to this problem which plagued the state making it difficult for the common man to even carry on normal daily functions. None of the educational institutions were functioning properly and the health care system was also severely affected during this time. However, the census in 2001 and 2011 was undertaken in the state of Jammu & Kashmir as a part of All India Programme.

The state of Jammu and Kashmir has a unique and peculiar topography which acts as a hindrance in achieving the desired goal of complete literacy or Universalization of literacy in the state. The network of schools is spread sparsely and the majority of population live in far flung and inaccessible areas, put up with many problems like lack of easy access to institutions, lack of infrastructure, weather vagaries and the like. The level of literacy is very low in state of Jammu & Kashmir making it one of the four States of India from the bottom in terms of literacy rate.

Also the literacy rate of urban areas has not shown satisfactory growth whereas the rural literacy rate has grown reasonably, thereby exhibiting an encouraging and increasing trend. The growth in the rural literacy can mainly be attributed to increasing number of educational institutions which have almost doubled from last two decades in the state.

In order to enhance the level of literacy, a basket of initiatives in the form of interventions, were introduced to develop this core indicator of human development. With the help of these target oriented interventions, the number of educational institutions was increased which resulted in maximum area coverage and decreased the average area per school covered.

Literacy - National Comparison

The strong focus on the Universalization of basic education and health in the 10th and 11th Five Year Plans reflect a visible shift in the approach towards development planning and recognized that though the major indicators of socio-economic development viz., growth rate, birth rate, death rate, infant and maternal mortality rate and literacy rate are interlinked, the literacy rate is the major determinant of the rise and fall of other indicators.

Trend of literacy rate at state level

The literacy rate at state level has increased from 11.03 percent (16.97 percent males and 4.26 percent females) as per census 1961 to 68.74 percent (68.26 percent males and 58.01 percent females) as per census 2011 showing an increase of 57.71 percentage points over the five decades i.e., from 1961 to 2011.The gender literacy gap has also decreased in the same time period. The literacy rate for the census year 2011 has been calculated for everyone who is '7 years and above in age'.

Literacy in J&K has made remarkable strides since 1961, which is supported by the results of census 2011. It is not only the literacy rate which have made progression over the time but the absolute figures of literacy have increased remarkably exhibiting its strong presence both in rural and urban areas of the State.

Gender disparity in literacy is historical phenomenon. In 1961, while literacy rate for males was 16.97 percent, it was only 4.26 percent in case of females. The gap in literacy was 12.71 percentage points in favour of males. This large disparity still continues in male/female literacy situation. While about three fourth of the males in the state are literate in 2011, the landmark of 50 percent has only recently been achieved in the case of females. The gender gap in literacy rates has increased from 12.71 percentage points in 1961 to 23.93 percentage points in 2001, however as it has decreased from 23.93 percentage points to 10.25 percentage points in 2011 exhibiting the convergence of literacy rates to some extent. This is an indication of improvement of female literacy and the rising importance of the education of girl child in this country.

However, the micro-analysis of the facts show contrary and encouraging results as far as female literacy is concerned. The female literacy at both Rural and Urban has shown higher growth in literacy than males. The highest progression has been made by rural females whereas least progression by urban males.

The analysis has brought this fact to the fore that the efforts put in by the government through various interventions to reach to the rural areas (especially far flung areas) and bring down literacy gap have started materializing at ground level and there is a hope of greater convergence of literacy status through rural and urban areas and especially among male and female as well.

There is a large urban-rural differential in literacy rate. This differential was of the order of about 22 percentage points during 2001 and has continued to remain so over the last several decades. It has come down to 15 percentage points during 2008. While more than three-fourth of urban population is literate, literacy rate in rural areas is still below the two-third mark. Literacy rate for females in rural areas is still lower, being only 52.70 percent. When it is compared to the literacy rate of 83.15 percent for urban male population, the gender and rural-urban disparities become glaring evident.

Education is an instrument of social change. It empowers individuals and communities, generates an awareness of one's own potentialities and inner strengths equipping people to combat oppression, exclusion and discrimination. This survey which aims to study the literacy rate in the South Kashmir region since independence was done sex-wise, rural–urban and age-wise. Therefore, the data of literacy growth in South Kashmir has been broken down and arranged according to the decade and district. From 1948-1979 there was only one district in South Kashmir region namely Anantnag. In 1979 South Kashmir was divided into two districts carving out a separate district of Pulwama. In 2007, South Kashmir was divided into four districts viz, Anantnag was further divided to make Kulgam and Pulwama was divided to create Shopian.

Table No. 4.26: Showing the Sex-wise literacy rate of India from 1951-2011

Census year	Literacy rate in percentage points	Sex-wise		Gender literacy gap	Decadal literacy growth in males	Decadal literacy growth in females	Overall decadal literacy growth
		Male	Female				
1951	18.33	27.16	0.86	26.3	N.A	N.A	N.A
1961	28.03	40.04	15.35	24.69	12.88	14.49	9.7
1971	34.45	45.96	21.97	23.99	5.92	6.62	6.42
1981	43.57	56.38	29.76	26.62	10.42	7.79	9.12
1991	52.21	64.13	39.29	24.84	7.75	9.53	8.64
2001	64.83	75.26	53.67	21.59	11.13	14.38	12.62
2011	74.04	82.14	65.46	16.68	6.88	11.79	9.21

Source: Census Hand Book of Government of India.

Note: NA = Not Available

The above table shows the statistics about the sex wise literacy rate in India from the years 1951-2011. The table shows a continuous growth in the literacy rate in all aspects after our independence. We can also observe that the gender literacy gap has been decreasing steadily which shows the growing importance of education of girl child in our country.

118

Table No. 4.27: Showing the sex-wise literacy rate of Jammu &Kashmir from 1951-2011

Year	Literacy rate in percentage points	Sex-wise		Gender literacy gap	Decadal literacy growth in males	Decadal literacy growth in females	Overall decadal literacy growth
		Male	Female				
1951	N.A	N.A	N.A	N.A	N.A	N.A	N.A
1961	11.03	16.97	4.26	12.71	N.A	N.Z	N.A
1971	18.58	26.75	9.28	17.47	9.78	5.02	7.55
1981	26.17	35.49	15.82	19.67	8.74	6.54	7.59
1991	N.A	N.A	N.A	N.A	N.A	N.A	N.A
2001	54.46	65.75	41.82	23.93	N.A	N.A	N.A
2011	68.74	68.26	58.01	10.25	2.51	16.19	14.28

Source: Digest of Statistics, Directorate of Economics & Statistics, Government of J&K and Census Hand Books of Government of India.

Note: NA = Not Available

The above table shows the statistics about the sex wise literacy rate in the state of Jammu and Kashmir. There was no census conducted in the state of Jammu and Kashmir in the year 1951. After that continuous census was conducted with the exception of 1991 when the census recording could not take place due to the militancy activity being widespread in the region during this time. On an analysis of the above table we can see a continuous growth in the literacy rate as well as a decrease in the gender literacy gap. The state of Jammu and Kashmir is lagging behind in the literacy rate as compared to the national average which shows us that there is a huge scope for improvement in the future.

Table No. 4.28: Showing the sex-wise literacy rate of South Kashmir from 1951-2011

Census year	Literacy rate in percentage points	Sex-wise		Gender literacy gap	Decadal literacy growth in males	Decadal literacy growth in females	Overall decadal literacy growth
		Male	Female				
1951	N.A	N.A	N.A	N.A	N.A	N.A	N.A
1961	8.04	13.69	1.47	12.22	N.A	N.A	N.A
1971	14.98	23.60	4.81	18.79	9.91	3.34	6.94
1981	21.60	31.90	10.07	21.83	8.3	5.26	6.62
1991	N.A	N.A	N.A	N.A	N.A	N.A	N.A
2001	47.76	59.04	38.95	20.09	N.A	N.A	N.A
2011	63.55	73.54	53.10	20.44	14.5	14.15	15.79

Source: Digest of Statistics, Directorate of Economics & Statistics, Government of J&K and Census Hand Books of Government of India.
Note: NA = Not Available

The above table shows the statistics about the sex-wise literacy rate in the South Kashmir region. The above table shows that there was an increase in the literacy rate of South Kashmir from 8.04% in 1961 to 63.55% in 2011. The overall literacy rate of South Kashmir region even today is less than the literacy rate of state of Jammu and Kashmir and also that of the national average. The highest decadal increase was in the year 2011 overall. We can observe that the gender literacy gap has increased from 1961-1981 there has been an improvement which can be seen from 2001.

Table No. 4.29: Showing the rural-urban literacy rate of South Kashmir from 1951-2011

Census year	Persons	Rural	Urban	Rural urban literacy gap	Rural decadal literacy growth	Urban decadal literacy growth
1951	N.A	N.A	N.A	N.A	N.A	N.A
1961	8.04	7.40	17.00	9.6	N.A	N.A
1971	14.98	13.80	28.10	14.3	6.4	11.1
1981	21.60	20.27	37.41	17.14	6.47	9.31
1991	N.A	N.A	N.A	N.A	N.A	N.A
2001	47.76	45.25	57.82	12.57	N.A	N.A
2011	63.55	61.73	72.69	10.96	16.48	14.87

Source: Digest of Statistics, Directorate of Economics & Statistics, Government of J&K and Census Hand Books of Government of India.
Note: NA = Not Available

The above table shows the relative figures for literacy in the rural and urban areas of South Kashmir. We can see that the rural-urban literacy gap has been widening from 9.6 in 1961 to 17.14 in 1981, and after that there was a slight improvement in 2001 where it dropped to 12.57 and in 2011 it dropped to 10.96. This shows that the education is still out of reach for large population which lives in the rural as well as tribal areas. The reason for this being no private schools in these regions and also the lack of basic facilities in the public schools which are situated in these areas.

MAJOR FINDINGS OF THE ABOVE SECTION

While analysing the data, it was found that there was no census conducted in the state of Jammu and Kashmir in the year 1951. After that continuous census was conducted with the exception of 1991 when the census recording could not take place due to the militancy activity being widespread in the region during this time. On the basis of analysis it was found that there is growth in the literacy rate and decrease in the gender literacy gap in south Kashmir. It was found that there was an increase in the literacy rate of South Kashmir from 8.04% to 63.55% from 1961- 2011. The overall literacy rate of South Kashmir region even today is less than the literacy rate of state of Jammu and Kashmir and also that of the national average. The highest decadal increase was in the year 2011 overall. It can be observed that though the gender literacy gap has increased from 1961- 1981, there has been an improvement which can be seen from 2001. It was found that the rural-urban literacy gap has been widening from 9.6 to 17.14 from 1961- 1981, and after that there was a slight improvement in 2001 where it dropped to 12.57 and in 2011 it dropped to 10.96. This shows that the education is still out of reach for large population which lives in the rural as well as tribal areas. The reason for this being no private schools in these regions and also the lack of basic facilities in the public schools which are situated in these areas.

SECTION – F
IMPACT OF EDUCATION ON DIFFERENT STRUCTURES OF SOCIETY

In the contemporary world, education is an important tool for every citizen to succeed, as it mitigates the challenges which we face in life. The knowledge gained through education enables the individuals' potential to be optimally utilized which is due to the training of the human mind to think in a rational and analytical manner. This opens doors of opportunities and also enables the individual to achieve better prospects in career growth. Education has always played a paramount role in the modern industrial world. The foundation of the society in this age is based on education since it brings economic and social prosperity and this enables them to run a modern society. The current advancement in technology has been influenced largely by education, as individuals are able to apply the skills acquired in real life leading to innovations. Also the employment in the contemporary world is based on this aspect, as employees must possess the required skills that correspond with the current technology to perform their tasks. Education also has a great social importance especially in the modern, complex industrialized societies and it is essential for everyone. Education in today's world also helps people earn respect and recognition. As a matter of fact, everything we create today is based on the knowledge that we obtain throughout our life by way of education. It assists scientists in inventing equipment and devices, resulting in a new technology nowadays. The more developed life becomes, the more necessary education is for everyone. Education has played a major role in the development of post-independence India and put in a league of developed countries. The same has also played a major role in how Kashmir has changed in the past 60 years. The situation in South Kashmir is not different and the education has played a major role in influencing the lives of people and changed the different structures of the society in the region. Education had a larger role to play in changing the face of way the society today embraces issues like women education, employment, marriages and the status of children and women in the family. It has also played a major role in changing the socio economic conditions of the people as well as influenced the sectors like healthcare, tourism, infrastructural facilities, sanitation and general public welfare.

Impact of education on the literacy in South Kashmir region

The initial effort to get a census for the first time in the year 1891, after that regular census were conducted till1941. In 1951, the circumstances in the state were not conductive for conducting the census. In 1961, 1971 and 1981 the censuses were taken as a component of the census of India. No census was conducted during 1991 due to administrative complications which can generally be familiar to the dilemma of militancy being at its pinnacle throughout this era which made the usual running of administrative functions difficult. Nevertheless, the census in 2001 and 2011 was undertaken in the state of Jammu & Kashmir as a element of All India Programme.

Education is an instrument of social change. It empowers individuals and communities, generates an awareness of one's own potentialities and inner strengths equipping people to combat oppression, exclusion and discrimination. This survey which aims to study the literacy rate in the South Kashmir region since independence was done gender-wise. Therefore, the data of literacy growth in South Kashmir has been broken down and arranged according to the decades.

The analysis has brought this fact to the fore that the efforts put in by the Government through various interventions to reach to the rural areas (especially far flung areas) and bring down literacy gap have started materializing at ground level and there is a hope of greater convergence of literacy status through rural and urban areas and especially among male and female as well. The literacy growth rate of the South Kashmir is presented below in tabular form and figures:

Table No. 4.30: Gender-wise literacy rate of South Kashmir from 1951-2011

Census year	Literacy rate in percentage points	Gender-Wise		Gender literacy gap	Decadal literacy growth in males	Decadal literacy growth in females	Overall decadal literacy growth
		Male	Female				
1951	N.A	N.A	N.A	N.A	N.A	N.A	N.A
1961	8.04	13.69	1.47	12.22	N.A	N.A	N.A
1971	14.98	23.60	4.81	18.79	9.91	3.34	6.94
1981	21.60	31.90	10.07	21.83	8.3	5.26	6.62
1991	N.A	N.A	N.A	N.A	N.A	N.A	N.A
2001	47.76	59.04	38.95	20.09	N.A	N.A	N.A
2011	63.55	73.54	53.10	20.44	14.5	14.15	15.79

Source: Digest of Statistics, Directorate of Economics & Statistics, Government of J&K and Census Hand Books of Government of India.
Note: NA = Not Available

The above table shows the statistics about the gender-wise literacy rate in the South Kashmir region. The above table shows that there was an increase in the literacy rate of South Kashmir from 8.04% in 1961 to 63.55% in 2011. The overall literacy rate of South Kashmir region even today is less than the literacy rate of state of Jammu and Kashmir and also that of the national average. The highest decadal increase was in the year 2011 overall. We can observe that the gender literacy gap has increased from 1961-1981 and there has been an improvement which can be seen from the year 2001. The above changes show that there has been an improvement in literacy rate due to the increased awareness about education among the people.

Impact of education on the enrolment of students in schools, colleges and other institutions of learning

Table No. 4.31: Showing the total number of students enrolled in schools, colleges and other institutions of learning in South Kashmir from 1948 to 2013

Year	Total number of students enrolled at elementary level	Total number of students enrolled at secondary level	Total number of students enrolled at college level	Total number of students enrolled in other learning institutions
1948	11596	3942	00	13
1951	22398	6424	86	173
1961	41615	8394	171	526
1971	56734	13976	455	945
1981	94358	20218	941	1843
1991	127682	40339	2981	3013
2001	151634	64023	9669	5249
2011	238174	130147	32390	9393
2012	240277	136349	34479	10541
2013	239083	138301	34971	12854

Source: Field Survey

The above table shows the enrolment numbers in the different levels of education in the South Kashmir region from 1948 to 2013. It also shows that there has been a steady increase in the enrolment from 1948 to 2013 in all the levels. The table depicts that more number of people is taking interest in getting education due to the increased awareness about the advantages it brings about.

Impact of education on health

Education is widely held to be a key determinant of fertility and infant health. From a theoretical perspective, several causal channels have been emphasized. First, education raises a woman's permanent income through earnings, tilting her optimal fertility choices toward fewer offspring of higher quality. Second, education may improve an individual's knowledge of, and ability to process information regarding, fertility options and healthy pregnancy behaviours. Education could improve health through at least the following channels: raising efficiency in health production (productive efficiency), changing inputs in health production (allocate efficiency), changing time preference, changing behavioural patterns, e.g. smoking, obesity, preventive care and finally, gaining more resources, e.g., higher income, occupational status, better housing, better food, better quality of care, and living environment. There is abundant evidence on the associations between education and health, whether health is measured by mortality, morbidity, or health behaviours. International comparative studies have documented that the associations exist in multiple countries, although magnitudes might differ, if the association is causal, then the effect of education on health should be taken into account when forming education and health policies.

In the State of Jammu and Kashmir birth rate, death rate, fertility rate and infant mortality rate of the state is less than all India indicators with higher percentage of institutional delivery and full immunisation. As compared to 22.5 birth rate at national level, J&K has 18.3 birth rate which was 23.4 in 2000-2005 followed by 5.7 death rate which was 7.7 in 2000-2005, fertility rate which was 2.8 in 2000-2005 and infant mortality rate which was 73.2 in 2000-2005 as compared to 7.3 per cent, 2.6 per cent and 47 per cent respectively at all India level. Similarly, as compared to 72.90 per cent institutional delivery at the all India level and 67.2 per cent safe delivery, 61 per cent full immunisation and 71.5 per cent children vaccinated with DPT, J&K has 80.9 per cent, 82.9 per cent, 66.6 per cent and 77 per cent respectively. The life expectancy in the state is 66.5 years which was in 63 years in 2000-2005 for males and for females the same is 69.3 which were 64.5 years in 2000-2005, both are higher than that of the national average.

Fertility planning: Fertility continues to decline in Jammu & Kashmir. At current fertility level women will have an average of 2.71 children each throughout their child bearing years. Among women 25-49 yrs, the median age at first birth is now 20.3 years, one year higher than the national average and women age 15-19 account for only 8 percent of total fertility. In Jammu & Kashmir 88% of women want at least one son and 83% of women want at least one daughter. Knowledge of contraception is virtually universal. In Jammu & Kashmir while 49% rural respondents live in villages that are electrified; only 6% live in villages that have a cable connection. 58 percent married women listen to the radio at least once a week, 55% of women watch television at least once a week which gives them better awareness about the changes in the society and also encourages them to gather knowledge about the recent advancements in the field of technology, healthcare, sanitation and education systems.

Infant mortality: Jammu and Kashmir has fared better than any other states in the country with regard to the Infant Mortality Rate. In 2013, the state recorded an Infant Mortality rate (IMR) of 37 as compared to the national average of 40. "The infant mortality rate in the state has come down from 39 in 2012 to 37 in 2013 and is recorded better than the national average of 40 as revealed by latest data of Sample Registration System 2014 bulletin.

Impact of education on print media

There is no denial in the argument that print media is one of the oldest medium of news delivery and is still going best despite coming into being of number of other modern, faster and better electronic mediums of news delivery. The industry is very well organized across the length and breadth of globe, wherein readership taste has been always taken care of. The industry has always adhered and fulfilled its basic aim & purpose, to keep general masses informed about the developments taking place in and around the society they dwell in. Newspaper industry is perhaps one of the largest in the world which has started publishing its content in hybrid form, viz. both print and online version and either way the aim is to not to lose the readership at any cost and even if there is loss on one front it should be gained on another front. In the year 1964 only one title was registered from the state of Jammu & Kashmir with RNI which can be also considered as the beginning of era of newspaper industry in state. Except for the year 1965 titles were registered each year thereafter till 2013.

The valley of Kashmir did not have any English daily and Jammu had two small newspapers before the eruption of anti-India insurgency in the state in 1989. The scene is different today as around 30 big and small English dailies are published from Srinagar and Jammu cities, where nearly one-fourth of Jammu and Kashmir's 10 million population lives.

The newspaper market is flourishing in Jammu and Kashmir as the Indian State strides ahead in its fight against illiteracy. According to Jammu and Kashmir Government's information department, around 150 newspapers in different languages hit the stands every morning in Srinagar and Jammu, the state's summer and winter capitals, respectively. This is in addition to 200 weekly newspaper and 150 fortnightly and monthly publications, while dozens of persons, according to an official of the information department, apply for new titles every month. Among the prominent permanent newspapers are Greater Kashmir, Kashmir Times, Daily Excelsior and Rising Kashmir all in English.

Urdu is official language of Muslim-majority Jammu and Kashmir and it boasts of dozens of newspaper like Daily Aftab, Srinagar Times, Daily Alsafa, Kashmir Uzma, Udaan and Taskeen. Monthly English political magazines like 'Conveyor' and 'Honour' launched almost simultaneously along with weekly Kashmir life a couple of years ago have also earned a committed reader ship. And the number of publications is increasing day by day.

Jammu and Srinagar are the two capital districts of the state of Jammu and Kashmir and are also the home of maximum number of newspapers and periodicals, given this fact one can clearly argue that urban areas especially the state headquarters are the hub of publishing industry.

Owing to fact that there is constant and continuous increase in the registration of new titles with the Registrar Newspapers for India (RNI), one can easily refute any immediate potential threat to the print media in the state of Jammu & Kashmir. Jammu and Srinagar being the two capital headquarters of the state have emerged as the two largest newspaper publishing districts of the state in their standing order in almost every respect. Although, Urdu, Kashmiri and Dogri are the official languages of the state of Jammu & Kashmir, but it is the Urdu language which enjoys more popularity over the other two official languages. Publishing periodicals in 10 different languages across the 22 districts of the state speaks about the linguistic diversity of Jammu & Kashmir. Technology has bought revolution in many ways and newspaper publishing industry is no exception to it. Without any denial, technology is efficient in many ways and delivering faster and accurate information and overcoming the barriers of space and time. Most of the newspapers have adapted to hybrid publishing only to uphold the interest of their readers and not to lose their patronage. Public arguments towards the approaching death of print newspapers got refuted from time to time, whether when correlated with the coming into being of electronic gadgets like Radio, TV etc to the present day internet. As of now one can argue that there is no approaching death to print media in general and in the state of Jammu & Kashmir in particular when internet has penetrated only up to 34.3% population at global level and 11.4% in India.

Impact of education on the empowerment of Kashmiri women

Women Empowerment is a global issue and discussion on women political rights are at the fore front of many formal and informal campaigns worldwide. The concept of women empowerment was introduced at the international women conference at Nairobi in 1985. Education is a milestone in women empowerment because it enables them to respond to the challenges, to confront their traditional role in the society and also change their lifestyle so that we can't neglect the importance of education in reference to women empowerment. In the recent years, the empowerment of women has been recognized as the central issue in determining the status of women. The National Commission of Women was set up by an Act of Parliament in 1990 to safeguard the rights and legal entitlements of women. The 73rd and 74th Amendments (1993) to the constitution of India have provided for reservation of seats in the local bodies of Panchayats and Municipalities for women, laying a strong foundation for their participation in decision making at the local level.

The decades after independence have witnessed tremendous changes in the status of women in the state of Jammu and Kashmir. The constitution has laid down as a fundamental right the equality of sexes. Revolutionary changes have taken place in the

130

position of women after independence. The Constitution of India provided for special steps to be taken by the government to improve the condition of women by separate institutions. A quick and effective change in the status of women was contemplated through social legislations. The Constitution guarantees certain fundamental rights and freedom such as protection of life and personal liberty. Women are the beneficiaries of these rights in the same manner as men. Article 14 ensures equality before law and Article 15 prohibits any discrimination. Article 16(a) forbids discrimination in any respect of employment of office under the state on the grounds only of religion caste, sex, descent, and place of birth, residence or any of them.

The western society encouraged women to come out of their homes to earn like men. Kashmiri women, like women in other places, too were being affected by these changes. The mass change among Kashmiri women started from early 20th century. While the upper class women responded early and fully to the changing processes, other women belonging to lower socio-economic groups responded to the change very late.

The women were deprived of their rights, but reminded of their duties. But with the changing times, the role of women changed from only a child bearing and rearing machine to the bread earner too. Due to the rapid growth of industrialization and modernization, urbanization, development in the field of transport and communication, improvement in science and technology, not only new roles for the women emerged, but also new social norms and values developed. The women started getting education and showed interest in the political and professional fields. Besides, the other areas of social living, they began to come out of the domestic spheres and took professional roles outside their homes. This helped them to realize their potentialities, broaden their outlook and create a new meaning for themselves. The traditional role of a house wife gradually evolved into the dual and more fulfilling role of professional working wife and thus housewife, at the same time.

Thus the Kashmiri women have undergone a significant degree of change in the fields of education, profession, nutrition and health. Education including technical and professional education started now for women from primary to university level. They started to be employed in services, establishment, offices and professional and technical occupations. They have now entered into occupations and professions formerly practised and dominated by men. Consequently, more and more Kashmiri women have not only stepped out of their traditional roles to slip into the world of work but have silently and surely made sizeable in roads into the traditional male bastion. Education, economic liberalization has thrown open a new world of market opportunities for women which has played a great role in bringing the women of Kashmir, to adopt medical profession as well for the last more than two decades. Now women are awakened to their talents and realize the social responsibilities. Women are aware of the new trends and their own rights. The important reasons for their adopting the medical profession are their desire for higher status, economic self-sufficiency utilization of individual talent, to secure equality in terms of status, self-confidence, satisfaction, development of potential and personality. Besides, the educational status of parents has motivated the women to adopt medical profession. The changes in their positions and roles have brought along with them changing attitudes, behaviour patterns and the emerging problems related to medical profession. It is mostly through women's own talent, scientific knowledge and attitude, excellent academic records and women's inclination and interest in modern professions including medical profession, that the Kashmiri women of today have reached the present climax.

MAJOR FINDINGS OF THE ABOVE SECTION

The above discussion shows us vividly the numerous positive changes that education has brought about in the state of Jammu and Kashmir and South Kashmir in particular. Education has had a positive impact on people realising the benefits of it, thereby encouraging more people to have good education which can be seen in the increase of literacy rate and enrolment numbers. Education also had a large impact on the healthcare, sanitation and the general wellbeing of the people of the Jammu and Kashmir. With increased access to education and which in turn gives them access to the best practices, people have started taking more preventive measures. Also print media had a very large role to play in changing the way perceive things in the valley. Due to more number of people getting education, their appetite for information has also increased; this can be seen through the rising number of print media publications in the state. Also education had a very large role to play on the changing status of women in the state. Education has brought about awareness and now women have a larger role to play in the society. They now even have almost equal social status and they are no longer only a child bearing machine but are playing a major role in technical, medical, financial and educational sectors. They are also fast becoming the bread winners of the family. Thus education played a major role in realizing their own potential and working towards their goals and it has also encouraged more women to get education which is shown in the earlier chapters that there is lesser gender gap in enrolment these days. Thus, education had a very large role to play in removing the gender barriers and also sensitising the people about the changes taking place around the world.

Recommendations

Inferential suggestions

In the light of the present study the following suggestions have been put forth:

1. The present study revealed that the public schools lag behind the private schools. So, there is a need to overhaul the system especially in public sector in order to make it more accountable and making provisions for encouraging competent, honest and dedicated teachers by meaningful rewards etc.

2. Initiating the attractive schemes (reinforcement) in government schools to expose the students to the outside world by making provisions for out of state tours which may help in solving the problem of retention at the elementary level.

3. Making provisions for special training courses for government as well as private teachers especially developing in them the motivation skills so that advanced techniques of the teaching may be inculcated in them.

4. To establish a system wherein the pass percentage of the students can be used to give suitable rewards to the teachers and also to give them adequate feedback and inputs in their teaching.

5. The government should take steps to reduce the drop out percentage happening when students take admission into secondary and higher secondary levels. Special emphasis should be made to get more girl children to complete their higher secondary education.

6. To improve the quality of government secondary schools in academics and co curricular activities.

7. A full-fledged university with a wide range of courses may be opened in the South Kashmir while keeping in view population and the distance of the area from the main campus of Kashmir University. Besides professional colleges for the women is the need of the hour keeping in view the social scenario of the Kashmir society?

8. So far as the literacy rate of South Kashmir is concerned, it is lagging behind the State of Jammu and Kashmir. The department of human resource development must take some major steps to overcome and make education possible for each and every child of the state. The second thing is that there should be centres of guidance and counselling for the general public for conveying the message about the benefits, merits of education as well as literacy. And there should be more separate girl schools with full educational facilities particularly in rural areas which are still educationally backward as compared to the urban areas of South Kashmir and the rest of the state.

Suggestions for further research

No research is complete in itself. The present study is also not an exception and opens up avenues for further research, which are briefly mentioned below:

1. The present investigation was confined only to South Kashmir region of Jammu and Kashmir. It can be further extended to other regions of the state.

2. The research was confined to study the education and institutions of learning in the South Kashmir region. Same study can be conducted for the development of education among schedule caste/ schedule tribe, orphans, women education etc.

References

Administrative Reforms Commission. (1968). *Report of the Machinery for Planning*, Government of India, New Delhi.

Aggarwal, A.K. (2005). *Development of Education System in India.* Anmol Publication Pvt. Ltd.

Aggarwal, I.P. (1986). Some Economic Aspects of School Education; A comparative study of government and private Schools in Delhi, District wise, *DEPA, NIEPA,* New Delhi.

Aggarwal, J.C. (1961). *Selected Questions on Education,* Delhi: Doaba House.

Aggarwal, J.C. (1966). *Major Recommendations of the Education Commission,* Arya Book Depot, New Delhi.

Aggarwal, J.C. (2002). *Landmarks in the History of Modern Indian Education,* Visas Publishing House Pvt. Ltd., New Delhi.

Aggarwal, Yash. (1998). Primary education in Delhi, How much do the children learn? *National Institute of Educational recently & Administration*, New Delhi.

Aiyar, S.P. (1966). Perspective of the Welfare State (Ed.), *P.C. Manktala and Sons* Pvt. Ltd.

Akangtemba (1986). Development of Primary Education in Mokokchung District, Nagaland. M.A. Dissertation, 1986, NEHU, Nagaland Campus, NEHU, Kohima. pp.47.

Ali, A.A. (1972*).* Education Reform in Kashmir: An Approach, *Inquiry,* 1(3).

Allen, J. and Others (1965). *The Cambridge Shorter History of India,* S. Chand and Company, New Delhi.

Altekar, A.S. (1943). *Education in Ancient India,* New Delhi: Motilal Banarsidass.

Angrist, et al. (2002). Vouchers for Private Schooling in Colombia: Evidence from a Randomized Natural Experiment. *The American Economic Review,* **92** (5): 1535-1558.

Anwar J., (1988). A Comparative Study of the Problem Experienced by Secondary School Teachers under different Management in Andra Pradesh and their Impact on the Performance of Students. Ph.D. Education. Osmania University.

Appadorai, A. (1968). Integration Council and its Task. *The Hindustan Times*, June 20.

Appleby, Paul H. (1953). Public Administration in India: *Report of a Survey* (New Delhi, Manager of Publications).

Archer, R.L. (1912). *Rousseau on Education,* New York, Longmans, Green and Co.

Arnstine, Donald. (1967). Philosophy of Education: Learning and Schooling, New York, Harper and Row.

Aster Fessehassion. (1989). Women, War and Peace, *Research Report* No. 14, Uppsala, Life and Peace Institute.

Attekar, A.S. (1974). *Education in Ancient India,* Motilal Banarasi Dass, Varanasi.

Babukuttan, P. (1997). *A study on existing inspection and supervision of primary school of Kollan District,* Kerala: DEPA.

Bamzai, P.N.K. (1962*). A History of Kashmir,* Metropolitan Book Co. Private Ltd, Delhi.

Barro R, Lee JW. (2001). International Data on Educational Attainment, *Updates and Implications, Oxford Economic Papers,* **53**(3): 541-563.

Bashir A. Dabla, Sandeep Nayak, Khurshid-ul- Islam. (2000). Gender Discrimination in the Kashmir valley, *Gyan Publishing House, New Delhi.*

Basttle, Jean Allen. (1969).Culture and Education for the Contemporary World, *Columbus, Ohio,* C.E. Merrill Publishing Co.

Basu, A.N. (1952). Indian Education in Parliamentary Papers, *Part-I* (Asia Publishing House, Bombay).

Basu, A.N. (1947).Education in Modern India, *Orient Book Co,* Calcutta.

Bazaz-Prem Nath. (1959). Daughters of the Vitasta, *Pamposh Publications,* New Delhi.

Beloff, M. (1953). The Federal Solution in its Application to Europe, Asia and Africa, Political Studies-I.

Bentley, T. (1998). Learning Beyond the Classroom, *Education for a Changing World,* London, Routledge.

Bernier, Dr. Francois. (1914). *Travels in the Moughal Empire.* Oxford University Press.

Bettinger, Eric. (2005). Private School Vouchers in Colobia. *In Harvard University and World Bank Conference on Mobilizing Public Sector for Private Education,* Cambridge: Massachussets.

Bhagwan Dayal. (1963). *The Development of Modern Indian Education,* Orient Longmans, Bombay.

Bhargava, M.L. (1958). *History of Secondary Education in UP,* Suptdt. Printing and Stationery, UP, Lucknow.

Bhatnagar, R.P. and Verma, I.B. (1978). *Educational Administration,* Loyal Book Depot, Meerut.

Bhatnagar, Suresh (1971). *Kothari Commission: Recommendations and Evaluation,* Loyal Book Depot, Meerut.

Bhatnagav, Suresh (2000). *Indian Education: Today and Tomorrow,* International Publishing House, Meerut.

Bhatt, B.D. and J.C. Aggarwal, (1969).*Educational Documents in India* (1913-1968) (Arya Book Depot, New Delhi).

Bhattacharjee B. (1981-1982). A Study of the Planning and Financing in respect of the Secondary Education of Meghalaya. *M.Ed Dissertation. NEHU,* Shillong.

Biddle, Brue J. et al. (1966). *Essays on the Social System of Education,* Columbia, Missouri, University of Missouri.

Birdi, B., (1992). *Fifth survey of Educational research* 1988 -92 (vol. 1), pp. 294 NCERT.

Biscoe, C.E.T. (1925). *Kashmir in Sunlight and Shade,* Seeley Service and Co., London.

Blackman C., (2004) *Paying the Price*: the Future for Europe's Media Sector. Foresight 6: 292-301.

Blackwell, Fritz (2004). India: *A Global Studies Handbook,* United States of America: ABC-CLIO, Inc.

Bomar Behram (1943). *Educational Controversies in India,* Bombay, D.B. Taraporevala, p.633.

Bombwall, K.R., (1979).*Foundations of Political Science* (NCERT, New Delhi).

Boud, D. and Miller, N. (1997): *Working with Experience*: Animating learning, London, Routledge.

138

Brar, S.K. (1998). *A Comparative Study of the functioning of Government and Private Schools of the Faridkot District* – Punjab, Unpublished Diploma Dissertation, NUEPA, New Delhi.

Brookover, W.B. (1955). *Sociology of Education*, New York, American Book Co.

Brubacher, John S. (1950). *Modern Philosophies of Education*, McGraw Hill Book Company, INC, New York.

Buhler, Sir, George (1875). *Detailed Report of a tour in search of Sanskrit Manuscripts made in Kashmir*, Rajasthan and Central India Trubner and Co., London.

Burns, H.W. (Ed.), (1963).*Education and the Development of Nation*, Syracuse, Syracuse University Press.

Butler, J. Donald (1968). *Four philosophies and their practice in education and religion.* New York & London: Harper and Row.

Byrne, Bridget, (1996) *Towards a Gendered Understanding of Conflict*, IDS Bulletin,

Cale, Luella (1950). *A History of Education: Socrates on Montessori*, New York: Holt, Rinehart & Winston, Inc.

Carras, Mary C. (1979). *Indira Gandhi in the Crucible of Leadership*; Boston, Beacon Press.

Cenkner, William (1983).*A Tradition of Teachers*: Sankara and the Jagadgurus Today, Delhi, MotilalBanarsidass.

Census Reports of India (J&K) 1941, 1951, 1971, 1981, 2001 and 2011. Directorate of Statistics and Economics, Government of Jammu and Kashmir, Srinagar.

Challenge of Education (1985). A Policy Perspective Ministry of Education, Government of India August.

Chanda, Ashok K.(1965)., Federalism in India, (George Allen and Unwin, London).

Chandra Kumar Singh (2006). *A Comparative Study of the Government and Private Schools at Elementary Education in Imphal Municipal Block.* Manipur, Unpublished Diploma Dissertation, NUEPA New Delhi.

Chatterjee, Sir Jagdish Chander (1914).*Kashmir Saivaism Research Department, Srinagar.*

Chatterji, Amiya, (1971).*The Central Financing of State Plans in the Indian Federation* (K.L. Mukhopadhyaya, Calcutta).

Chaubey, S.P. (1988). *History and Problems of Indian Education*, Vinod PustakMandir Agra.

Ciano, JN, (1987). *An investigation into the causes, effects & extent of wastage in secondary schools of Nairobi City: Kenya* – Dissertation for IDEPA through NIEPA.

Connell, W.F., Debus, R.L. and Niblett, W.R. (1967). *Readings in the Foundations of Education,* London: Routledge and Kegan Paul.

Dabla B. A. (1999). *Impact of Conflict situation on women and children in Kashmir,* Save the Children Fund, North West India, Srinagar.

Damle, Y.B. (1966). *Socialisation for an Unknown Future - Paper Presented to the Seminar on Higher Education, Technology and Social Change* (December 1-3, 1966). New Delhi, Indian Institute of Technology, Department of Humanities and Social Sciences.

Das, S.K. (1930). *Educational System of Ancient Hindus*, 152, Panchamon Tola Road, Calcutta.

Deighton, Lee C (1971). *The Encyclopaedia of Education*, Vol. I. The Macmillan Company and the Free press, New York.

Deka B. N. (1991). *Secondary Education of Assam with reference to Darrang District: An Analytical Study.* Unpublished Ph.D. Thesis. Department of Education, NEHU, Shillong.

Desai, A.R. (1966). *Social Background of Indian Nationalism*, Bombay, Popular, Prakasthan.

Deutsch, Martin, (1964*).Early Social Environment: It's Influence on School Adaptation, in The Social Dropout, Washington, National Education Association.*

Devi, R. (1985). *Barriers in Primary Education of Scheduled Caste Students*, Buch Vol. IV, p. 1268.

Devraja, N.K. (1963). *Philosophy of Culture*, Kitab Mahal, Allahabad.

Dewan, R., (1972). *Female Education in J&K State*, Unpublished M.Phil Dissertation, University of Jammu.

Dewey, John, (1939).*Democracy and Education: An Introduction to Philosophy of Education,* New York, G.P., Putnam's Sons.

Donaldson, Gordon A (2001). *Cultivating Leadership in Schools,* New York, College Press.

Drew, Fedrich (1877). *The Norther Barrier of India,* Edward Standford London.

Dube, S.C., (1977). *India Since Independence*: Social Report on India (1947-1972 Edited), New Delhi: Vikas Publishing House Pvt. Ltd.

Dupuis, A.M. (1972). *Philosophy of Education in historical perspective.* New Delhi: Thomson Press (India) Ltd.

Duraisamy Malathy (1996). *Demand for & access to child school in T.N,* UNOP studies on Development.

Duraismay, Malathy (1999). *Cost, Quality and Outcomes of Primary Schooling in Rural Tamil Nadu:* Does School Management Matter? Indian Educational Review, Vol. XXX, No. 2.

Dyer, C. & Choksi, A. (1997). *The demand for education among the Rabaris of Kutch,* West India, Nomadic Peoples, 1 (2).

Eddings, Jerelyn , (1994) *Role of Women in Decision-Making in the Peace Process,* in S. Wölte, ed., Human Rights Violations against Women during War and Conflict, Geneva, Women's International League for Peace and Freedom.

Education Policy Statement (1955). Ranbir Govt. Press, Jammu.

Educational Information in India Since 1998: *Education in Jammu and Kashmir online available at*: http://www.bestindiaedu.com/jammu-and-kashmir.html

Educational Innovations for Development, A.P.E.I.D., Vol.III, No.2, NCERT, New Delhi, December, 1986.

Educational Statistics at a Glance, Department of Education, J&K State, 1982.

Edwardes, Michael, British India (1772-1947), (Rupa and Company, Calcutta), 1976.

EFA Global Monitoring Report (2007). UNESCO, Paris.

Eisenstadt, S.N. (1956). From Generation to Generation, Chicago, Free Press.

Elder, Joseph W. (2006). *Caste System, Encyclopaedia of India* (vol. 1) edited by Stanley Wolpert, 223–229, Thomson Gale: ISBN 0-684-31350-2.

Elementary Education in India Analytical Report (2003). National University of Education Planning and Administration New Delhi.

Emerson, D.K. (1968). *Students and Politics in Developing Nations*, London, Paul Mal.

Erickson, Erik, H.P. (1970). *Gandhi's Truth: On the Origins of Militant Nonviolence*, New York, Norton.

Eron, Leonard D., et al., (1963). *Social Class: Parental Punishment for Aggression and Child Aggression, Child Development*, vol. xxxiv, No.4.

Final Population Totals (Scheduled Castes) 1981; Directorate of Census Operations, G.O.I., 1982.

Fordham, P. Holland, D. and Millican, J. (1995). *Adult Literacy, A Handbook for Development Workers,* Oxford, Oxfam.

Franda, Mercus F. (1968). West Bengal and Federalising Process in India,

Fuller, Bruce (1987). *What School Factors Raise Achievement in the Third World?* Review of Educational Research 57 (3):255-292.

Gandhi, M.K. (1957). *Basic Education (Ed. by Bharatan Kumarappa)* - Ahmedabad, Navajivan Publishing House.

Ganesha H.S. Bhatia, (1989). *Secondary Education: A System Approach*. Ph.D. Thesis. Department of Education, University of Mysore, Mysore, 37.

Garforth, E.W. (1963). *Education and Social Purpose*, London, Old burire.

Ghachem L (2011). *Online Branding in Newspapers*: A conceptual Model. IBIMA Publishing.

Gledhill, Allan. (1964). *The Republic of India: The Development, Its Laws and Constitution* (London, Stevens).

GMR (2010). *Reaching the marginalized. Education for All Global Monitoring Report* 2010, Paris: UNESCO.

Goel, B.S., (1966). *Caste and Class Tension in Indian Education*, Conspectus (New Delhi, Indian International Centre, Vol., No.4).

Good, C.V. (1973). *Dictionary of Education,* McGraw Hill, New York.

Gordan A (2003). *The discourse structure of book reviews in Ghanaian Newspapers* (1950-2006). The Dawn Journal 2: 256-273.

Gore, M.S., Desai, I.P. and Chitnis, Suma (1967). *Papers in Sociology of Education in India,* New Delhi, National Council of Educational Research and Training,

Government of India, (1962). *Emotional Integration Committee:* Preliminary Report, New Delhi, Ministry of Education.

Government of India, Report of the University Education Commission (1948-49) (Manager of Publications), Delhi.

Govinda and Varghese (1991). *The quality of Basic Education Services in India,* A case study of Primary Schooling in Madhya Pradesh, A Collaborative Study by IIEP Paris and NIEPA New Delhi.

Govinda. R., (2002). *India Education Report, National Institute of Educational Planning and Administration,* Oxford University Press,

Govt of J&K General Department Notification dated 21st October, 1969 Unpublished, Department of Education.

Gul S, Islam S (2013). *Adoption of Social Media by online Newspapers of Kashmir.* Annals of Library and Information Studies 60: 56-63.

Gulala (1981, 1982, 1983). *Kashmir University Magazine.* University of Kashmir, Hazratbal Srinagar.

Hailu A. F; (1997). *A study of quality of secondary schooling in southern region in Eritrea* – A dissertation for IDEPA through NIEPA.

Hanson, A.H., (1966). *The Process of Planning:* A Study of India's Five-Year Plans (1950-1964), Oxford University Press, London.

Harley, Ruth, E., (1959). *Sex-Role Pressures and the Socialisation of the Male Child, Psychological Reports,* vol. v.

Harman, Wiliam (1989). *The Sacred Marriage of a Hindu Goddess,* Blomington, Indiana University Press.

Hartog, P. (1939). *Some Aspects of Indian Education: Past and Present,* London, Oxford, p.109.

Henia A., (1988). *A study of the growth and development of Education in Manipur* (1947 - 1968). Ph.D. Education, Jawaharlal Nehru University Fifth Survey of Education Research 1988, 1992. Volume II, published by NCERT (2000); p.81-82.

Henry, Nelson (1955). *Modern Philosophies and Education, the Fifty fourth year book of the National Society for the Study of Education, Part one*, Central Book Depot, Allahabad.

Hensen, Donald, A. (1967). *The Responsibility of Sociology and Education*, in On Education: Sociological Perspectives, Donald A. Hansen and Joel E. Gerstl (eds.), New York, John Wiley and Sons, p.22.

Holms, Brain (1967). *Education Policy & Mission Schools* (edited) Routledge & Kegan Paul London.

Howard, A. Ozmon & Samuel, M. Graver (1981). *Philosophical Foundation of Education*. London: Charles E. Merrill Publishing Company.

Hughes, A.G. and Hughes E.H. (1960). *Education: Some Fundamental Problems*, Longmans, Green and Co. Ltd.

Human Development Report (HDR). Paints Grim Picture of Literary Scenario, Kashmir Observer, India 13 July 2008.

Husen, Trosten, (1956).*Home Background and Behaviour in the Classroom Situation*, Research Bulletin, No.5, Stockholm Institute of Education, University of Stockholm.

Hussain, Yusuf: (1957).*Glimpses of Medieval Indian Culture*, Asia Publishing House, Bombay.

Hussain, Zakir (1959). *Educational Reconstruction in India* - New Delhi, Ministry of Information and Broadcasting.

India (2009).A Reference Annual (53rd edition), New Delhi: Additional Director General (ADG), Publications Division, Ministry of Information and Broadcasting, Government of India.

India, Ministry of Education, 1958, Indian University Administration: Report of a Conference of Vice-Chancellors (Delhi).

India, National Council of Educational Research and Training 1963-64, Physics, The Physical Sciences Study Committee Text on High School Physics (Delhi).

India, National Council of Educational Research and Training, Review of Education in India: 1947-61, Ministry of Education, New Delhi, 1961.

144

India, Post-War Education Development in India, Report by the Central Advisory Board of Education, New Delhi, January 1944.

India, Report of the National Committee on Women's' Education, Ministry of Education, Government of India, 1959.

India, Report of the University Education Commission 1948-49, Vol. I, Government of India Press, Simla.

J&K, Report of the Sayah Committee on Education, Ranbir Press, Jammu, 1972

Jafar (1936). Education in Muslim India, Macmillan Co., London.

Jagger, J.D. (1989). Primary School Headship and the Appraisal of Head Teachers, unpublished M.Ed. Thesis, University of Leeds.

Jain, S.N. (Ed.), (1972). The Union and the States (National Publishing House, Delhi),

Jala J., (1986.). An Investigation into the Development of Secondary Education in Meghalaya since Independence. Ph.D. Thesis. Department of Education, NEHU, Shillong.

James, H.R. (1917).Education and Statesmanship in India, Bombay, Longmans.

Jammu and Kashmir Government Education Institutions Improvement Fund Rules, 1976 Unpublished, Department of Education, J&K.

Jayasuriya, J.E (1980). Education in Korea: A Third World Success Story, Colombo, Associated Educational Publishers.

Jesselyn, Irene M. (1965). The Happy Child, New York, Random House.

Johari, J.C. (1982). *Comparative Politics,* Sterling Publishers Pvt. Ltd., New Delhi.

John V.V. (1973). *Misadventures in Higher Education*, Young Asia Publications, New Delhi.

Johnson R, Gutierrez A (2010). Reinventing the business model of the newspaper industry: electronic business models and the newspaper industry. *The Wall Street Journal as case study.*

Johnson TJ, Kaye BK (2004). Wag the Blog: How reliance on traditional media and the Internet influence perceptions of credibility of Weblogs among Blog users. *Journalism & Mass Communication Quarterly* **81**: 622-642.

Johnson, W.L., and Snyder K.J. (1987). Instruction Leadership Training Needs for School Principals. *Journal of Educational Administration,* **24**(2) 1987 pp. 237-253.

Kapur, M.M. (1972). Education in J&K State, Department of Education, J&K State,

Katz, Joseph (1974). Education in Cana (Archon Books, Hamden, Connecticut),

Kaul Bhatia, Ashima, (2000). Valley of victims, Times of India, 7 July.

Kaul, J.N. (1975). Higher Education, Social Change and National Development, Indian Institute of Advanced Study, Simla.

Kaura S.P. (1973). *A Critical Study of the Development of Secondary Education in Punjab since the Year 1947.* Ph.D. Thesis. Chandigarh: Punjab University,

Kazami, A.A. (1952). Report of educational reorganisation in the Jammu & Kashmir State.

Kerlinger, F.N. (1983). Foundation of Behavioural Research, Delhi: surjeet publications Ministry of Human Resource Development.

Khanday, Zamrooda, (2004). *Women in Kashmir: negotiating for life;* Women's Global Network for Reproductive Rights Newsletter. No. 1.

Khongwir C. (1990). *Contributions of St. Anthony's School Shillong to the Development of Education in Meghalaya.* Unpublished Dissertation, NEHU, Shillong.

Kingdon G-G (2007). *The Progress of School Education In India,* Global Poverty Research Group Website: http://www.gprg.org/ the work was part of the programme of the ESRC Global Poverty Research Group.

Kingdon, Geeta Gandhi, (1996). *Private schooling in India: size, nature and equity effects, a research study financed by the Ford foundation; The development Economics Research Programme,* London school of Economic and Political Science, London.

Kiran Bhatty, (1998). Educational Deprivation in India. A survey of field Investigations, *Economic and Political Weekly,* Vol.33, No.27, pp.1738

Kirk, Robert N., (1965). Educating Slum Children in London, School and Society Vol.93, No.2250.

Knowles, A S. and Jossey, (1977). *International Encyclopaedia of Higher Education* (Ed.). Jossey-Bass Publishers San Francisco.

Kohli, Santa: (1977). *Family Planning in India: A Descriptive Analysis,* New Delhi, Indian Institute of Public Administration.

Kothari, D.S.(1962). Some Aspects of University Education, U.G.C. Delhi.

Krishna, G. (1986). An investigation into the academic performance of students (Boys & Girls) at the secondary & Sr. Secondary stage, in the schools under different Management in the Union Territory of Delhi – a dissertation for DEPA - NIEPA New Delhi.

Kulkarni, N.B. (1982). *Inspection and Supervision of primary schools in Maharastra region with special reference to Marthawada region;* Ph.D (Education) study, Poona University.

Kundu, C.L. (1979). *Indian Year Book on Teacher Education,* Sterling Publishers, New Delhi.

Kupinsky, S. Ed. (1977). *The Fertility of Working Women:* A Synthesis of International Research, New Delhi, Praeger.

Lambert, W.E. (1966). *Children's Views of Foreign Peoples;* A Cross-national Study, New York, Appleton-Century-Crofts.

Lawrence, W.R. (1895). *The Valley of Kashmir,* Henery Frowder London.

Lingappa, K.R., (1958). *A Challenge to Social Education, Bangalore,* The B D.D. Power Press.

Lokmanya Shikshak, (1991). *A Journal of Education, Rajasthan Vidyapith,* Udaipur, vol.15.

Lucas Robert (1988). *On the Mechanics of Economic Development,* J. Monet. Econ. 22.

Ludden, David (1985). *Peasant History in South India,* Princeton, Princeton University Press

Luniya, B.N. (1975). *Evolution of Indian Culture,* Lakshmi Narain Agarwal Education Publishers, Agra.

Lyndem B. (1985). *A Critical Study of the Development Plans: Programmes in Primary Education in the State of Meghalaya since Independence.* Ph.D. Thesis. Department of Education, NEHU, Shillong.

Majumdar T.R., (1988). *A Study on Secondary School of Education in Calcutta: A Study of the Total System.* Ph.D. Thesis. Department of Education, Calcutta University, Calcutta.

Malhotra, Sudha (1998). *A Study on Enrolment, Attendance and Retention in Primary School in Primary Schools in relation to incentives schemes*, Allahabad, U.P: Innovative Research Association.

Mathur, V.S. (1968). *Studies in Indian Education*, Arya Book Depot, New Delhi.

Mehar R., B.S. Dhillon and M.S. Sarkaria (2007). Performance Differentials of Male and Female Students in Relation to Habitation, Type of Schools and Subject Combinations at the 12th Stage in Districts Amritsar and Gurdaspur, *Recent Researches in Education and Psychology*.

Mehta, Prayag, (1969). *Achievement Motivation in High School Students*, New Delhi, NCERT.

Mehta, T.S. and Chandra, R. (1972). *Population Education*: Selected Readings, National Council of Educational Research and Training.

MHRD, 1984, 1986, 1988, 1992, 1998, 2000, Publication Division, Government of India, New Delhi.

Ministry of Education, Central Advisory board of Education (1935-1960). Silver Jubilee Souvenir, New Delhi, 1960.

Mishra, K.S. (1993). *Education for Exploring Policy Issues*, Chugh Publications, Allahabad.

Misra, B.R. (1963). *Indian Federal Finance,* (Orient Longmans, Calcutta).

Mitra, Ved (1964). *Education in Ancient Indian,* Arya Book Depot.

Moorcraft, William (1841). *Travels in the Punjab Ladakh and Kashmir* etc. John Murray London.

Morgan, V. (1992). Head teachers in a new Context: Integrated Schools in Northern Ireland, *Cambridge Journal of Education,* 22 (2) pp. 215-226.

Morris-Jones, W.H., (1964). *The Government and Politics of India.* Hutchinson, London.

Mudhuliar (1952). *Education Report on Secondary Education in India.* Superintendent Publications, Delhi.

Mukherjee, R.K. (1970). *Ancient Indian Education*, S. Chand and Co., New Delhi.

Mukherji, S.N. (1980). *Education in India: Today and Tomorrow*, Acharya Book Depot, Baroda.

148

Muniswamy, C. (1991). *Mushroom growth of private English medium schools in Karnataka. Who is to be blamed? How to curb it?* A case study of Bangalore South district, DEPA, NIEPA, New Delhi.

Musson RMW (1986). The use of newspaper data in historical earthquake studies. Disasters 10: 217-223.

Myrdal, Gunnar, Asian Drama (1972). *An Enquiry into the Poverty of Nations* (Abridged Edition) Penguin Press, London.

Naik, J.P. (1965). Educational Planning in India, Allied Publishers, Bombay.

Naik, J.P. (1970). Union-State Relations in Education: Their implications for Educational Administration. *The Indian Journal of Public Administration,* Vol.XVI, No.3.

Naik, J.P. (1975). *Policy and Performance in Indian Education,* Orient Longman, New Delhi.

Naik, J.P. (1990). *Instructional and Nurturant Effects of Jurisprudential Inquiry Model of Teaching,* Unpublished doctoral thesis, University of Allahabad,

National Council for Teacher Education (NCTE) Act, 1993.

National Curriculum for Elementary and Secondary Education: A Framework, 1985.

National Policy on Education (1986). With modifications undertaken in 1992.

National Staff College for Educational Planners and Administrators, 3rd All India Survey of Education: Jammu and Kashmir, 1978.

Natrajan. J. (1989). *A study in the Planning & Management of Libraries in Govt. High School & Higher Secondary Schools of Pondicherry* - A dissertation for DEPA – NIEPA, New Delhi.

Nautiyal (2001). *A study of Socio-economic problem in enrolment and retention of Muslim Girls in Primary level* at Roorkee block of district Haridwar and Uttaranchal.

Nurullah Syed and Naik, J.P. (1955). *A Student History of Education*, MacMillan Co., India Limited, Bombay.

Omvedt, Gail(1993). *Reinventing Revolution: New Social Movements and the Socialist Tradition in India*, New York, Sharpe.

Palkhivala, N.A. (1994). *We, the Nation,* U.B.S. Publishers Distributors, Ltd., New Delhi.

Pandey, R.S. (1996). *Education in Emerging Indian Society*, Vinod Pustak Mandir, Agra.

Pandey, R.S. (1992). National Policy on Education in India, Horizon, Allahabad,

Pandit, R.S. (1935). *River of Kings* - (Translation of Kalhana's Raj Trangini in English) Indian Press Allahabad.

Pandita, Ramesh (2012). *Growing Use of Electronic Sources of Information* – A User Survey of Baba Ghulam Shah Badshah (BGSB) University. Trends in Information Management 8: 43-51.

Pandita, Ramesh (2013). Electronic Documents: An Integral Component of Teaching Learning Process: A Critical Evaluation. *E-library Science Research Journal,* 1: 31-37.

Paranjape, H.K. (1963). Political and Administrative Problems of Implementing the Indian Plan, *Indian Journal of Public Administration,* Vol.IX, No.4.

Parohit P, (1989). *A Study of the Role of the Secondary School Teachers Organisation in Relation to the Qualitative Improvement of Secondary Education in Orissa after Independence,* Ph.D. Thesis. Department of Education, Utkal University. Cuttack.

Passi, B.K. and Singh, P. (1991). *Value Education,* Agra: National Psychological Corporation.

Pati S., (1992). *A Study of the Administrative and Supervisory Problems of Secondary School Headmaster of Cuttack-I Circle.* M. Phil. Dissertation. Department of Education. Utkal University.

Pigozzi, M. J. (1999). *Education in Emergencies and for Reconstruction:* A Developmental Approach. United Nations Children`s Fund, Program Division Education, Document No. UNICEF/PD/ED/99-1.

Planning Commission (1955). *Social Welfare in India-* Delhi, Publications, Division.

Poignent R. (1966). *Social Change in Modern India,* Bombay, Allied Publishers.

Prabhu, Joseph (2006). *Educational Institutions and Philosophies, Traditional and Modern, Encyclopaedia of India* (vol. 2) edited by Stanley Wolpert, 23–28, Thomson Gale.

Probe Team, (1999). *Public Report on Basic Education.* Oxford University Press, New Delhi.

Provisional Population Totals (1982). Paper I J&K State 1981; Directorate of Census Operations, G.O.I.

Psacharopoulous G, Woodhall M (1985). Education for Development; An Analysis of Investment Choices. 108. *Univers. J. Edu. Gen. Stud.* Washington: World Bank.

R.K. Suri and Kalapana Rajaram (2008). *Infrastructure: Science and Technology in India,* edited by New Delhi: Spectrum.

Radha Kumud Mukherji (1951). *Ancient Indian Education Delhi,* Motilal Banarsidas,

Radhakrishnan S., (1949). Report on University Education Commission, Government of India.

Rai, B.C. (1977). *Problems of India Education,* Prakashan Kendra, Lucknow.

Rai, Lala Lajpat, (1968). *The Problems of National Education in India,* Delhi, Publications Division.

Rain L. (2005). Youth are leading the transition to a fully wired and mobile nation. Teens and Technology, Pew Internet and American Life Project, USA.

Raj Krishna, (1964). Thought on Tradition and Modernity, *Quest* (41).

Rajguru S.P. (2014) Research Directions, *International Multidisciplinary Research Journal.* Vol I Issue XI.

Rajput J.S. (1999). *Education in a Changing World-Practices and Forces,* Vikas Publishing House, New Delhi.

Ramamurthy, M.S. (1974). The *Constitutional Framework in the Higher Learning in India (Ed.),* by Amrik Singh, Vikas Publishing House, Delhi.

Raman, S.A. (2006). *Women's Education,* Encyclopaedia of India (vol. 4), edited by Stanley Wolpert, 235–239, Thomson Gale.

Ranson, S, & Stewart, J. (1994). *Management for the Public Domain;* New York, St. Martin's Press.

Rao, V.K. (1999). *Hand Book of Primary, Secondary and Higher Education,* Rajat Publications, Delhi.

Rasool G. & Minashi Chopra (1986). *Education in Jammu and Kashmir: Issues and Documents.* Jay Kay Book House, Residence Road Jammu Tawi.

Rath, Sharada, (1978). *Centre-State Relations in the Field of Social Services,* Oriental Publishers and Distributors, New Delhi.

Rawat, P.L. (1968). *History of Indian Education,* Ram Prasad and Sons, Agra.

Raza Moon, Ahmad A. and Nuna Schell C., (1990). *School Education in India.* The Regional Dimension, NIEPA, New Delhi.

Razdan, P.N., (1962). Progressive Education, Mahnoor, Srinagar

Recommendations for Newspapers Industry (2009). Newspapers Today.

Registrar of Newspapers for India (2013) Govt of India, New Delhi.

Rema N.K. (1986). A study on effectiveness of the role & involvement. Parent Teacher Association (PTA) in the high school of Badagara Educational District – Kerala – a dissertation for pre induction DEPA – NIEP New Delhi.

Report of the Backward Classes Commission (1969). Ranbir Govt. Press, Jammu.

Report of the Committee on Education Reorganization (1939). Ranbir Govt. Press, Jammu.

Report of the Education Commission (1964-66). Supplementary, Vol.II, Delhi, 1970.

Report of the Education Commission (1964-66): Education and National Development (Manager of publications), Delhi.

Report of the Education Conference on 10+2, 1975, NCERT New Delhi

Report of the Educational Reorganization Committee1950; Ranbir Govt. Press, Jammu.

Report of the Indian Education Commission, 1964-66; NCERT, New Delhi.

Report of the Jammu and Kashmir Inquiry Commission, 1969, Ranbir Govt Press, Jammu, 1969.

Report of the Jha Committee on Education, 1978. Unpublished Document, Ministry of Education, J&K.

Report of the Secondary Education Commission, 1953; G.O.I., Ministry of Education.

Report of the Sharp Committee on Education, 1916. Manager of Publications, G.O.I.

Report of the Study Group on the Training of District Education Officers, 1972, National Staff College for Education Planners and Administrators.

Report of the Task-Force on Education (1982) unpublished record of Jammu and Kashmir State Education Department.

Report on the Reorganization of Education Department by J.D. Sharma 1973Sharp Education Committee Report on Jammu and Kashmir 1916.

Roman, R.K: (1983). *A study on Inspection and Supervision of elementary schools in Phaileng,* Mizoram; NIEPA.

Saini, S.K. (1993). *Development of Education System in India.* Cosmo Publishers, New Delhi.

Saint CE (2012). Depression as a Journalism Subject: Exploring the Folha Groups Files (1970-2009). *Brazilian Journalism Research* 8: 160-175.

Saiyidain, G.A. (1938). Report on Reorganisation of Education in Jammu & Kashmir State.

Saiyidain, K.G. (1965). *Education: Science of Education,* Raj Kamal Prakashan, New Delhi.

Sarva Shiksha Abhiyan (2011-2012). Annual Work Plan and Budget (AWP&B) Report of Jammu and Kashmir.

Sathya, (2001). Politics behind the Purdah, Communalism Combat, November.

Sehgal, Rashme, (2003). Kashmiri village with only widows, Grassroots: Reporting the Human Condition 4(8).

Sen Gupta Piyali and Guha Jaba (2002). Enrolment, Dropout and Grade Completion of Girl Children in West Bengal, Economic and Political Weekly, Vol.37, No.17, pp 1621-1637.

Seru, S.L. (1973). *History and Growth of Education in Jammu and Kashmir: 1872-1973,* Ali Mohammad and Sons, Srinagar.

Setty, E.D. and Ross, E.L. (1987). A Case Study in Applied Education in Rural India, *Community Development Journal, Oxford University Press* 22 (2): 120–129.

Shadunsky A. (2011). Newspaper Stocks Deserve Another Look As Fundamentals Improve. Seeking Alpha.

Shakir, R.S. (1980). *Enrolment pattern of Government and Aided schools in Delhi,* Dissertation submitted to DEPA, NIEPA New Delhi.

Sharma K.J. (2008). *Participation in Elementary Education: A Comparative Study of Government and Private Unaided Schools in Bishnah Zone of Jammu District in Jammu and Kashmir.* Unpublished Diploma Dissertation, NUEPA, New Delhi.

Sharma, P. (2005). *Philosophy of Education.* New Delhi: A.P.H. Publications.

Sharma, R.A. (2003). *Teacher Training Technology,* R. Lall Book Depot, Meerut.

Sharma, R.A. (2004). *Development of Education System in India,* R. Lall Book Depot, Meerut.

Sharp, H. (1920). *Selections from Educational Records,* Part I (1781-1839). Superintendent, Govt. Printing, Calcutta.

Singh Shailendra and Sridhar K. Seetharsm (2002). Govt. and Private School: Trends in Enrolment and Retention, *Economic and Political Weekly,* Vol. 37, N. 4, pp.4229-4231-4233-4238.

Singh Y.P. (1998). Parishad vs. Private Schools: A Comparative Analysis, *Giri Institute of Development.*

Singh, P., (1985). To develop a mechanism for conducting organizational evaluation & diagnosis in Govt. Sr. Secondary School of Delhi – *A dissertation for DEPA – NIEPA New Delhi.*

Singh, R.P. (1972). *The Indian Public School,* Sterling Publishers Pvt. Ltd., New Delhi.

Singh, Raja Roy, (1963). Educational Administration in India, Administrative Reforms since Independence, *Supplemented to Indian Journal of Public Administration,* Vol.IX, No.3.

Singh, Suman K. and Kumar Sunil (1999). Private and Government Primary Schools: A Comparison in Rural setting, *Patna Bihar Education Project.*

Sinha, R.K. (1990). *Alienation among Scheduled Castes,* Manas Prakashan, Delhi.

Solanki K.N., (1992). A Study of the Relationship between the Educational Management and the Organisational Climate of the Secondary Schools of Saurashtra Region. Ph.D. Thesis. Department of Education, Saurashtra University, Surat.

Sonalde Desai Amaresh Dubey Reeve Vanneman and Rukmini Banerji (2008). Private Schooling in India: A New Educational Landscape, *India Human Development Survey Working Paper No.* 11.

154

Sripati, V and Thiruvengadam, A.K. (2004). India: Constitutional Amendment Making The Right to Education a Fundamental Right, *International Journal of Constitutional Law,* 2 (1): 148–158, Oxford University Press.

Srivastava Ravi, Panchamukhi P.R, Shrivastava Ranjana (2005). *Universalizing Elementary Education in India,* Uncaging the Tiger Economy, Oxford University Press.

Srivastava, R.C. (1973). *Theory and Practice of Teacher Education in India,* Chug Publications, Allahabad.

Stein, Sir M.A. (1900). *Kalhana's Rajtarangeni - Translated into English,* Archibald Constable & Co., London.

Sterling J. (2008). *A plan for a US newspaper industry counterattack against disruptive innovators.* Strategy & Leadership 36: 20-26.

Sufi Dr. G.M.D. (1949). Kashir, Vol.I and II, *The Punjab University press, Lahore.*

Suri Kavita, (2010). *Turtuk Unveiled,* Shubhi Publication, New Delhi.

Suri, Kavita, (2007). *Kashmiri women as peacemakers; Grassroots:* Reporting the Human Condition.

Talang D.H., (1992). *The Contribution of Seng Khasi Schools to the Development of Education in Meghalaya.* Unpublished Dissertation. NEHU, Shillong.

Tamjenkaba, (1993). *Development of Education in Nagaland in Post Independence period.* Unpublished Thesis for the Degree of Doctor of Philosophy, NEHU, Nagaland, pp. 322-324.

Tandon, Prakash: Punjabi Century, (1857-1947). *Berkeley,* University of California Press, 1968.

Taneja, V.R, (1980). Educational Thought and Practice (Revised and Enlarged Edition - Fourth Edition), Sterling Publishing Pvt. Ltd., New Delhi.

Thapar, Romila (1961). *Ashoka and the Decine of the Mauryas,* London, Oxford University Press.

The Constitution of Jammu and Kashmir, Academy of Art, Culture and Languages, 1969. Unpublished, Department of Education, J&K.

The Jammu and Kashmir Private Education Institutes Grants-in-Aid Rules, 1974; Unpublished, Deptt. of Education, J&K.

Thomas, Edward, J.(1927). *The Life of Buddha as Legend and History,* London, Routledge and Kegan Paul.

Trevelyan, Sir George Otto (1876). *The Life and Letters of Lord Macaulay,* Oxford University Press, Oxford.

Tsurmi, E. Patricia: (1984). *Colonial Education in Korea and Taiwan,* Princeton, Princeton University Press.

UNESCO. (2000). *Dakar Framework for Action: Education for All; Meeting our Collective Commitments.* Paris: UNESCO Publishing.

University Grants Commission (1976). Journal of Higher Education, Vol.2, autumn,

University News, Special Issue December 18-19, 1987 Association of Indian Universities, New Delhi.

Upanasani N.K., Choudhuri K., Deshpande V.S., Deshpande S.S., and Katre S.A., (1991). *A Study of Some Model Efficient and Inefficient Administration and Management at the Secondary School level in Pune District: Independence Study.* Ph.D. Thesis. Pune University.

Vincent, S.R., (1983). *The grant – in – aid,* codes as instruments to control private schools, DEPA, NIEPA, New Delhi.

Vrat, Prem (2006). *Indian Institutes of Technology,* Encyclopaedia of India (vol. 2) edited by Stanley Wolpert, 229–231, Thomson Gale.

Vyas G.L. (1984). A Comparative study of Managerial skills of Headmasters of Govt. & recognized secondary & higher secondary schools in Rajasthan. A Dissertation for DEPA – NIEPA New Delhi.

Walia, J.S. (2003). *Development of Education System in India,* Paul Publishers, Punjab.

Wangu, M.L., (1971). Development of Education in Kashmir during the Period 1846 to 1947 AD, Historical Perspective, Inquiry, Vol.1 No.2.

Wangu, M.L., (1972). *Growth and Strides of Education in J&K,* Educational India, Vol. 39 No 2.

Wheare, K.C., (1950). *India's New Constitution Anaysed,* Allahabad Law Journal, Vol.48, No.6.

Williams, G. (1996). Paying for Education beyond Eighteen: An Examination of Issues and Options, *Council for Industry in Higher Education, London.*

Young, G.M. (1935). *Speeches by Lord Macaulay with the Minute on Indian Education,* Oxford University Press, London.

Zakir Hussain (1937). Wardha Education Committee Report - Hindustan Talimi Sangh, Seagoan - Wardha.

Zothanmawii, (2007). *A Comparative Study of the Functioning of Government and Private Higher Secondary Schools in Aizawl,* Mizoram, Unpublished Diploma Dissertation, NUEPA, New Delhi.

Zvelebil, Kamil V. (1992). *Companion Studies to the history of Tamil Literature,* Leiden, Brill.